Transitions
a story in verse

E. A. Johnson

Transitions
Copyright © 2021 E.A. Johnson
All Rights Reserved
Published by Unsolicited Press
Printed in the United States of America.
First Edition.

No part of this book may be used or reproduced in any manner whatsoever without written permission except in the case of brief quotations embodied in critical articles or reviews.

This collection is a work of fiction written in verse. Any relation to, or resemblance of, an individual or family is merely a matter of coincidence and should not be interpreted as malice or intent by the author.

Attention schools and businesses: for discounted copies on large orders, please contact the publisher directly.

For information contact:
Unsolicited Press
Portland, Oregon
www.unsolicitedpress.com
orders@unsolicitedpress.com
619-354-8005

Cover Design: Arturo Hernandez
Editor: S.R. Stewart

ISBN: 978-1-950730-78-0

Acknowledgements

I want to take a moment to recognize all the suicide victims, both survivors and otherwise. Specifically, to Ryan, Sayvon, Mike, and Nathan, all of whom took their own lives amid desperate situations, you are remembered by those who were left behind.

I also want to dedicate this to all those who find themselves in that desperate and dark place. Push through, take it from someone who knows, there is light when you come out of the darkness.

Table of Contents

AUGUST — 1
    TOMORROW'S TOMORROW — 2
    ADVICE — 4

SEPTEMBER — 7
    NEW SCHOOL—OLD SELF — 8
    LIFE REIMAGINED — 10
    PHOTOGRAPHY CLUB — 12
    THE WORLD ACCORDING TO JOY — 14
    RISING STORMS — 16
    FALLING ANGELS — 19

OCTOBER — 21
    EMPTY BOTTLES — 22
    SCRATCHES — 25
    FORGIVENESS — 29
    PLAYING DEFENSE — 32
    BREAKING POINTS — 35
    CANDY AND COSTUMES — 38

NOVEMBER — 43
    ANOTHER ROUND — 44
    BREAKING BREAD — 46
    FOCAL POINTS — 49
    COLORS — 51
    BUT NOW IN THE SILENCE — 53
    IT'S WHATEVER — 55

DECEMBER — 57
    LIQUID FREEDOM — 58
    THE PARTY — 61
    AFTERMATH — 64
    BETRAYAL — 68
    DARKNESS — 70
    ASHES OF A FALLEN STAR — 72

JANUARY — 75

Used to Be	76
A Mother's Love	77
Needs	78
Sleep	80
Unanswered	82
Numb	85
Not My Fault	87
Choices	90

FEBRUARY — 91

Therapy	92
Expectations	93
Coming Back	96
Whispers	100
Thunderheads	101
The Terms of Your Surrender	103

MARCH — 107

A New Normal	108
Talking It Out	110
Ordinary Day	112
Secrets	115
A Mother's Lament	116
Boys and Men	118

APRIL — 121

What is There to Say?	122
A Father's Song	123
Breathless	126
Mulligans	129
Apologies	131
The Hatchling	137

MAY — 139

Here's the Trick	140
Maker	142
Her	144
Liminal Moments	146
Lift	148

JUNE — 151

The Bell	152

PUDDLES	153
NOTE FROM THE AUTHOR	**155**
AUTHOR BIO	**157**

August

Tomorrow's Tomorrow

Laying on my bed
        alone
at the end of freedom

Phone clutched deftly in my hand—
        lifeline and garrot.
It *pings* me,
                telling me I have friends, and I matter.

Colorful images flash before me, a parade of curated lives
        Curated dreams
        Curated nightmares
of *friends* I haven't seen in months insistently pressuring me to listen
                                      and see
                                      and judge
                   myself
                                      but not them
                                      never them.
    While I sit alone dreaming of tomorrow and tomorrow and tomorrow
    A day when I may be more like them,
                more like their picturesque lives
            and phantom souls,
    When I can forget that I am here
                          alone
    on the last day before tomorrow and the rest of the days after that.

Another *ping* from my phone, another dreamy vision of life,
                        another reminder that I am less than them—
                        my life is less interesting, less fun—

And already I dread tomorrow's tomorrow, the talk of travels and parties,

        Parties that I was never invited to,
on the first day of classes, on the first day of high school.

Ping. A picture of the sun and laughter. *Ping.* A picture of people and fire. *Ping.* The ocean waves at sunset. *Ping.* Group selfie. *Ping.* Selfie. *Ping. Ping. Ping. Ping.*

        I join the herd of selfies,
            no good
      Another and another and another
            No. no. no.
      They look lame, look like I'm trying too hard,
           trying
                to be noticed
                to be cool
                to be the me that everyone will like
      This one—the lights good, I'm smiling, I look fun—
                                    #selfiesunday
          I look fun right?
          Will people think I'm lame 'cause I'm alone?
          Will people think I'm a loser?
          Will people think?
          Will people care?
          Comment?
          Do I want them to?

Ping. Ping. Comments. *Ping. Ping.*
    — "Cool pic" — #slob — #seeyousoon —
I didn't look at the background, my rooms a mess, my life's a mess
    — #whatnottowear — #hate — #stand^2bullies —

          Summer changes nothing.
          School will change nothing.

        Text a friend—a real friend—no answer.
1:00 am — sleep and dread tomorrow's tomorrow again.

Advice

       He sat me down this morning
       to tell me about his high school days
       decades ago, before the cell phone,
       and when computers were a luxury.
       He calls them the good-old-days,
       days that defined him, made him,
       Sports, friends, classes, grades
       none of the worries of adulthood

"Adulting you kids are calling it"
       he wants to be the cool dad,
       not cramp my style.

Ping. #adulting

"High school is a big moment
      in a young man's life"
          defining—he repeats
          deafening—I think

Ping. #future

"Keep up your grades"
      he didn't but I should
"Careful who you hang out with"
      he'd been arrested
"Don't do anything you're not ready for"
      —I'm not ready for high school

Ping. #stress

"Best days—best days"
his are behind him—mine are—

    Where are my best days?
    Are they here and now?
    Do you know the best day
              of your life
                when you live it
      or is it like some fog of mystery,
            lost in the ether
              waiting
          for you to see it
                    only after you've passed?

Like the exit we didn't take on the trip that should have been
                                              fun
but ended up with my parents arguing
                       arguing about why neither of them listened
                     each repeated the same tired phrases
                     in some forgotten dance
                     when they used to love each other
                     not just the idea of each other.

Ping. #problems

"Don't forget that."
      —didn't hear what *that* was
"No matter what, you can leave that at school."

Ping

September

New School—Old Self

A new school is like any school
        especially Freshman year.

Everyone knowing everyone
        and the only stranger
        is the one up front.

Rows of classrooms down the hall
        Rows of desks in the rooms
                Rows of students in the desks
                        Rows of eyes on the students
                              Rows of judgements in those eyes

Walking
    [into battle]
    into class
                knowing the things that we know
                    about ourselves
                    about our peers
                    about our place
                expected to forget about social rivalries
                                    social hierarchies
                                    social media
              and work together—present in front—stand up.

Sitting in the back is my friend,
                        a world away from me
    my seat in the front
    He is safe behind those eyes that see me—
Judge me.
    Eyes that remember last year's mistakes.

            Then she walks in—fresh blood—and the sharks that are my peers
smell it on her.
      She trips and falls,
dropping her books,
     her syllabi,
     her papers,
     her sweater
shed under the heat of unwanted attention.

     And everyone
laughs—Everyone laughs at the unfortunately
tripped girl who it is safe to laugh at because nobody knows her.

Sweeping her papers into a discordant pile, she
stands and looks
                sheepish
                strong
                hopeful
     and nobody helps.

Knowing the judging eyes,
stepping out of my own shadow,
        out of my own way.

Putting her books on her desk,
Handing her the discarded sweater,
Smiling
                in the awkward silence
                under the laughing judgement
                of my peers.

    "Why are you out of your seat?"
            —that's what the teacher notices
     And everyone one
laughs again.

Life Reimagined

Noise for noises sake
echoing across the room and the hall
                         the hell
of excited voices eating crappy food
       "Right of passage" my father would say.
       Ping. #bestdays
I refuse to be the loner again
            —loser again—
                         but my friends aren't here.

Jostled in the line *Ping.*
       Picture a girl falling on the first day of school
       #betteryouthanme
       #drunk

I look around the room,
            faces buried in the glowing screens
            talking with out hearing,
            walking with out looking,
            posting with out caring,

She sits
       alone in the middle of a table
       along in the middle of a crowd,
       head down, food pushed away.
I take my tray.

                The old me would sit by the window,
                    away from the jeers
                    away from the comments
                    looking outside, to bounded freedom

        I know who I don't want to be—

The old me was
        quiet,
        embarrassed,
        shy.

I walk
    to the middle of the table
    to the middle of the crowd
        She is sitting down,
        looking at her tray
I say hello.

The new me will be
        friendly
        helpful
        open

She smiles through her tears
    beneath her arms
    her cellphone glares a picture
                of a girl
                falling
                on the first day of school.

Photography Club

She walks by me every morning
her hair the scent of lilacs in the summer
her skin, sun kissed even in September
her smile comes easily
and in her eyes—her eyes
I see the rising of a thousand suns in those brown eyes
so deep so rich so vibrant
Her hair floats after her as she walks, so dark that it shines blue in the sunlight

I see her across the room, or down the hall, walking,
hips swaying
the light falling gently around her
despite the harshness
of the cheap fluorescent bulbs
that glare at the rest of us.

We talk. She laughs,
    her hand—
    a touch, gentle on my arm
    sends a shock through me,
    a shiver
and I am powerless before her.

                "I'm going to the photography club," her voice
                so beautiful men would go to war over it.
                "Why don't you join with me? It'll be fun."

I want to say yes, but I won't be that high school cliché
    joining things for a girl,
      even for her, for Joy
whose very name is the emotion her glance graces me.

    I want to spend time with her,
        she could be my subject and my muse
I should say yes, it's expected that I'd want to,
        but she won't mind if I don't
        the world according to Joy
Is a world without fault or shade or glare
        a word that holds you comfortably
        cradled in loving arms?
Nothing can sway her faith from the simple joyful pleasure.

    "I would," I lie, "but I have to get home on Thursdays—
        to help my dad—"
            Sit on the couch and watch tv
                "to work around the house—"
            I'm not sure how things get fixed at home,
                —he's really handy."
                He's never held a hammer.

Joy's smile lights the dimming empty hall.
                "Too bad, it would've been fun."
        Then she kisses my cheek and flutters away with my soul.

And as she leaves,
                the crowded jostling hallway
comes to vicious life, and I am pushed
                against a locker
                      by a passing senior
Only to hear the bell and realize
        I am late for class again.

And Joy, she has left to warm the light in another room.
        I don't care about any of that
            because
        I said no and she kissed me anyway.

The World According to Joy

If you want to be happy,
If you want to smile more,
If you want to know who you are and like that person
        then you need to let go of the judgment of others
        let go of the hopelessness that is high school
        and know in no uncertain terms that you are amazing.

    Joy looked at herself in the mirror
                and said those words again

Camera resting on her dresser,
        her lens with which to see the world
                to see herself
    resting—waiting—watching

Being behind the camera was safer for her anyway
        there she could hide, there she could see.

Her phone buzzed, rarer still since she turned off her notifications
of things she now knew she didn't want to see.

A text from him,
        she smiled,
               those she liked,

    her knight in dirty sneakers.

                                    movies tomorrow?
                                    you pick i pay.

Joy smiled easily with him
    he was her rock

    he was her calm
    he was her filter for the world of high school

        yes. you pick this time
        i picked the last two
        food?

She waited for his response,
                hated—loved waiting
                          knowing he was going to respond
    it was a pleasing pain
    that never lasted long.

                      FOOD!

Joy laughed, Joy smiled, Joy danced.

Rising Storms

The rumbling outside my window,
                                        the low rumble
stops abruptly. A slam, a muffled curse,

                                        deep and low,
                                                I wait to hear
scraping sounds in the kitchen,

                                                words
                                                before I leave my room
                                                take my chance.

He's going on again, another bad day,
damn manager
damn customers
damn machines
damn
      I know I shouldn't ask today, but I didn't ask
      yesterday
      or yesterday's yesterday
                                                I'm running out of tomorrows,

"No" I never asked anything, "I know what you're going to ask—"
                                                freedom?
                                                help?
                                                money?
                                                love?
"What happened to what I gave you last week?"
                                                A movie and coffee
                                                not the food I promised
                                                I'm always coming up short
                                        temperature dropping
"Spend it on her, right? Joy is it?"

                                        my breath
                                        of spring flowers
                                        make weathering the storm
                                        worth it
"Birthday present? Why should I buy her a present?
She's your girlfriend. Get a job—get your own money."
                              low pressure moving in
                                        but he won't let me
                                        focus on school
                                        best years—best.
               "Take this."
                                        mom steps in
"You're coddling him.   helping
Always coddling him. He'll never learn
                                              to find what love
means?
how to stand on his own two feet—to be a man."
                    "You used to buy me presents."
"With my own money. Money I earned"
                         thunder cracks
"Money I worked for. What's he done?"
                    "His job is school. Your rules."
                              lightning and wind
"You think I don't remember my rules?
No excuse for not pulling his weight around here."
                    "He does his chores."
                                        shuffling my feet on the rug
                                        I watch
                              gathering clouds
                                        and look for shelter
"Cores are not the same as work."
                                        when you're fourteen
               "Why don't you head up
               finish your homework.
               I'll be up to get you for dinner"
                                        and the voices sound different

                                        from what you're used to
                                        and you're not sure how to stop
                    the rain falling
Muffled sounds through the bedroom door
                    wind howling through the eaves
                                        making the home you knew forever
                                        feel like a stranger
                    Something snaps, crashes down
    The door opens
                    the storm blows itself out.
        "Don't worry. You do your share,
        He's—struggling at work
            —a good man.
                —trying his best.
            He's—"
But her right cheek is red
and her eyes are puffy.
The door closes again
                                        in the silence
                                        after the world
                                        shifts beneath you.

            But storms that bad
            leave lasting damage.

Falling Angels

The house is dark and silent under the moon
        when my teammates
        my brothers
        my friends
        drop me off
        and drive off into the night
        laughing at the jokes we share
Outside the world looks peaceful
        rose bushes still hold some of summer's grace
        bathed in moonlight as the air chills
        Towering over the roof,
        evergreens stand stoic
        guarding life through the cold
        winters coming on.
I see what the world sees:
        tidy family in a
        tidy cape on a
        tidy street in a
        tidy neighborhood in a
        tidy town
        tidy
I see what the world does not see
        paint is peeling just under the eves
        the planting bed is full of weeds
        a wheel on the lawnmower wobbles on a bent axil
        overstuffed basement overflowing to an
        overstuffed garage which can't protect
        the car that is on its last legs in the driveway.
Opening the door, I walk into the kitchen
        he's sitting at the table staring
        into an empty glass

        next to a half empty bottle
        on top of unopened mail
        calloused hands turning the
        delicate glass catching the faint moonlight
I close the door and he starts talking without looking up from his glass
        "I didn't mean to do it, you know that.
        I promise that it's not going to happen again.
        It's just been really hard at work.
        Then I come home and everyone needs something
        I never really get a break, you understand, don't you?
        I'd never hurt you or your mother."
I tell him I understand, it's not his fault, I'm sorry.
        But none of that is true
        I do not understand why he's been so angry
        He was never like this before, yelled but never hit
        And if it isn't his fault, whose fault is it?
        Mine, mom's, his boss's, the bottle's?
        I do feel sorry, the rest I tell him 'cause he needs to hear it.
He smiles a smile that doesn't smile
        He eyes the empty glass
        He grabs the half empty bottle
        Golden liquid sloshed over the edge
        Landing on the unopened envelopes
        He looks at me over the edge of the glass
        Tears are in his eyes, he wipes his cheeks
I head upstairs to my room to do my homework
        I'm not sure what just happened
        I don't know why he's crying
        I just know that when he drinks
        I need to stay out of his way because
        I always make him angry because he doesn't realize that
        I am not him.

October

Empty Bottles

Chores.
I hate chores, but doing them has kept dad off my back,
so—

    Empty the dishwasher,
    clean my room,
    take out the trash.
    Repeat.
    Empty the dishwasher,
    clean my room
    take out the trash—

The garage used to smell like metal and grease
    that was when he'd spend his weekends out here
    working on the car
    showing me how
        Check the tires
        Check the oil
        Check the belts and breaks
    to properly maintain a car
        Wash it regularly
        Clean it out
        Take pride in your possessions
    is to properly maintain a way of life
Now it smells cloyingly sweet,
                the solid smells of dirt and oil
washed away by the pile of empty bottle that gathers
    every week
    in the corner
    where he used to keep his ratchet set
    where he used to teach me about cars

                                        and life
                                        and women

            He likes his bottles now more
                                        than he likes working on the car
                                        than he likes spending time with me
            I put the trash in the barrel and go to the corner.
            I can still smell his aftershave here
                    still remember the time
                                he showed me how to rebuild a carburetor
                                the intricate pieces that he explained
                                as he disassembled,
                                placed the pieces carefully on the bench
                                        between us, cleaned, shining, drying
                                        before he let me turn to screws, tighten
                                        tight but not too tight,
                                        a careful hand on mine
                                        showing me, teaching moderation.
Now that smell is almost hidden,
                                beneath the wash of sickly sweet old bottles
                                washed like the memories of this room
                                under the lip of the bottles.

The bottles used to fit in the recycling bin,
                                        now piled around it
                                        emptied on Friday
                                        overflowing by Wednesday.
What is it about these bottles that he likes so much more—
                            more than the time we spent together
        Picking one up, the smell turns my stomach,
        but it must be good because he chose it
        chose it over us anyway.

The bottle touches my lips
            and the smell—
                        the smell overwhelms my senses

burns my eyes
and I think about tilting it back
trying
the last few drops left
to be like him
But I know that my parents would not approve
and instead I place it on the bottles
already toppling bottles
unable to keep their balance
on the once empty bin
the bin that will be empty again
only to be filled before the week is over
before we can catch our breath
as the flood of sickly sweet scents over-washes
the world I once knew
replacing it with one that I'm hopeless to fathom the depths
and stem the flood without washing
out to sea myself.

I leave the garage and in the kitchen
on the counter
sits a new bottle
glowing amber in the afternoon sun,
beside a glass catching rays, throwing them
in gleeful colors
around the room.
I can hear football on the tv in the other room
and I know that he is there
eyes red, breath rank
yelling passionately at the pictures that move
across the screen
while ignoring the rest of the world
unless it interrupts his worship.

Scratches

Math, history, English, science
    Each with homework
        Each feels top priority
            Each ignores the others,
and I have to do them all

      Ping. #homeworksucks

    to just
  scratch the surface
of what I'm supposed to learn today,
      and tomorrow,
        and tomorrow,
          and tomorrow's
            tomorrow
But the footfalls
    thundering up the stairs
        say that something else
           is more important,

      Ping. #privacy

and I am powerless to avoid the door to my room slamming open
    nothing gentle in the huffing behind me
    transfigured form of my once guide teacher.

"How can you be so careless?"

    I put my pencil down
    after placing the remainder
    on my tenth answer of

       tonight's math problems

Thunder rumbles through my room.
My chair is wrenched backward, turned

       The paper I'm working on
       torn and wrinkled now
       carelessly falls to the ground.

"I taught you better than that," the thunder growls,
and I am the tree swept up in the tornado
               of papers
                     and life
           and confusion
                           and—
The rough hand drags me to the stairs
       for a moment I'm afraid
           I'll fall
       teetering on the precipice
                               suspended breathless
                 in the unflinching grasp
       of the storm.

The world is righted, and I descend the stairs of my own power

       caught up again
               in the raging grasp
           dragged through the kitchen
                 deposited
           not gently
       in the garage
               beside the car
   that we used to work on
           when times were
                       different.

"How could you be so careless?"
         He points to the side of the car,
  "see what you did?"

   but I didn't do it,
        there's red paint on the scratch
      that glides down the fender,
         and I didn't do it.

"You're calling me a liar?"
    the storm
      takes my bike
   off the ground
     "probably did it coming in with this"
        I promise—
     "I'll show you a promise."
    the bike is deposited
      not gently
   outside the garage
        clattering
     to a stop
       by the rose bushes
   that have lost their color
"Get over here,"
    the hand on my collar
       is the storm—not my father
   he has never been rough
     "you're calling me a liar?"
        "After all I've done for you"
      "everything I've sacrificed"
         "so you could have"
  "everything that I never did"
       the hand was not gentle
         when it hit me
    and I fell back
       against the workbench

                              into the bottles
            my face stung from the contact
                        my eyes burned
                                    with hooded rage
                        at this stranger
                        in my father's skin.
                He stood numbly before me
        seemingly unsure on his feet,
                        but I feel my lip throbbing,
                and my face stings.
"I didn't mean to—"
his words are meaningless to me
                the blood drums in my ears
                        and my eyes are burning with tears
                                that are not for him to see
        "Don't—" he looks at the door
                        "—don't tell your mother."
"It was an accident"
                an accident
                                I didn't listen anymore
                I walked away,
                        the power of the storm was spent
                                and picked up my bike and saw
                the new scratches
                        in the once unblemished frame
        Running my fingers over the rough metal
                that was smooth when I put it away
                        just this afternoon
                so it wouldn't be in his way
                when he came home.

I would be home late—after

                        after my own

                                        storms.

Forgiveness

Sitting on the bench
        the field
                        empty
before me as the twilight falls
              the setting sun
        throwing bruises on the sky.
                      I touch my eye and wince.

Two years ago this summer,
        that was when
                    I wasn't quite thirteen
                    He took me camping
           just us.

On the way to our site,
                tucked in the woods by the lake,
      we got lost.
                  We laughed about it,
        wandering through the darkening woods
                    looking for a letter on a wooden sign
                          in a forest of wooden signs
knowing that if we walked far enough
            around the circle of the lake road
    we would
        eventually
                    find our way.
        When we did
    tired and sore from carrying our gear
              we laughed because the car,
    parked so carefully in a clearing,
was three sights away.
              And on that day,

  when the sky was bruised,
          we set up our tent
    unloaded our fishing poles
      and roasted marshmallows for dinner,
and we laughed
    because mom would never approve.

The dew settled on the field
    in front of me
and the wooden bench
      where I sat waiting for my turn to play
    surrounded by my friends
           who are more than friends
   felt cold and hard beneath me.

The next morning,
      before the sun came up
    with the grass still wet with due,
  we went fishing,
    wrapped in blankets
    on a creaking row boat
    hot chocolate in thermoses
    and worms in a styrofoam cup.
He showed me how to bait a hook
      piercing the wriggling body
        wrap around the hook
      and pierce again.
  Casting the line in the water
Then, he'd said, the real work began.

I waited for the stars to come out
         over the field
  waited for something to change
      the day felt so important.
    Homework that I wouldn't be doing
sat on my desk,

but the fields in starlight were a special place.

Waiting on the lake
                        in the rickety row boat
         for the fish that wouldn't bite
              and didn't matter
because I was with him, and we talked
                    pulled in empty lines
      re-baited and re-cast
            replacing the awkward silence
                      with a memory.

Playing Defense

"Your mother made dinner."
        I already ate with my friends
                people who want me around
                who listen
"Is that phone of your's broken?"
        Works fine, how's your's?
            I know I shouldn't say it, but—
                he deserves worse
                he is looking for reasons
                to be mad, to yell, to storm
                and I will give them to him
"Don't give me that attitude,"
            So I silently wait for the winds to blow
    Rumbles spread the air
    the pressure drops again
    I have things to do
    for school
        that will take me away from here
"Too good for us?"
    No
        I'm not the one who is never here
        never present unless
the winds are blowing now
as the sky turns a sickly shade
        My phone buzzes
        and I check my messages
        from people who pay attention
these storms don't send the rain anymore
hail now, devastated landscapes
        Joy's texts shelter my mind
        from inbound pressures

"Get off that damn thing when I'm taking to you."
    Yelling you mean
"I'll show you yelling."
  "I told him to go out
  with his friends
  tonight."
"Oh you did? Didn't tell me."
    The winds shift, ice forms in sheets
    hidden on once safe roads
      She didn't know I was going out
      I never told her.
  "So leave him alone,
  and let him do his work."
"You're telling me what to do now?"
    Gail force winds predicted
    all lose items should be tied down
    to prevent damage
     There are other places
        I can go
        where people talk
        Joy's family talks
        They sit down
        for dinner
        and smile and laugh
    Hail strikes. Glass shatters.
     Leaving the doors open
     Hoping someone will see inside
     See through the mirage
     that is my life, my lie
     and stop the transfigured figure
     that I don't know anymore.
"Where do you think you're going?"
  "Leave him alone."
    Thunder and hail
    Rain begins to fall
"How will he learn to be a man."

*Something that was whole
now lies broken.*

Breaking Points

A note scratched on the pad by the counter
    an unanswered text
        buzzing again to read it
    these things don't register
    in a world filled with constant noise
          Ping. Picture of a family dinner. #homecooking
    where every noise is another note
    in the symphony of other people's lives
    while the discordant tones do not sing for me.
          Ping. Picture of a new car. #happybirthday
My bruises are still healing,
        the sickly green draining from the face
             fell off my bike
        if they asked
                Ping. #betteryouthanme
                  Ping. #clutz
                    Ping. #sad
        if they didn't ask
           I didn't offer.
    He's gotten better
           about keeping them
        hidden
           arms and chest
           Doctor said it might be a concussion
        if they ask
        but they don't
        Ping. #loser
The note on the counter,
           in my mother's pinched script
      says they are at the hospital.
              broken leg at his work

I wish it was his arm,
then he couldn't hit
but at least I'll be able to
stay out of his reach.

    He was drunk
      always drunk
   I'm sure and
     careless

When they come home,
     I'm watching tv
   homework
done   undone
   if they ask,
   they don't
     His cast is pail white, chalky,
he seems to be in pain,
    real pain
      pain that reminds you that you are alive
      that other people are alive
      that people feel
  and on the counter
      he sets
       a little orange bottle
       of little white pills
        one or two pills
        four or six hours
    Next to it, sits his other bottle,
       quarter full of golden liquid
    They go upstairs,
      alone,
      I open the bottle
       the smell
        of smoke and honey
     I want to know

      why he needs it
      where he goes
      when he drinks
      who he becomes
But the only way
      to truly know someone
      [so my English teacher says]
      is to walk a mile in their shoes
So I will look for my father here
      in this room
      while he settles
      in his own
      but just a little
      so he doesn't miss it
in this bottle.

Candy and Costumes

The door bell rings again
                a ghost and
         a robot zombie pirate
      their father stands behind them smiling
        at the creativity and
            the bravery
of his precious little charges.

I drop candy in their orange plastic pumpkins
    and remember when Sean,
        my brother's kid
               wanted to be a wizard
        wearing his mother's dress
            and a stick from the back yard
                enlisted as his wand
     I hung my head that Halloween,
         as he pranced with joy through my neighborhood
      My youngest was an
              Army Man
         eager to please his father
      Look daddy, he smiled up at me
              from under a mop of brown hair,
           look at my gun.
         His eyes always looking
                   for acceptance
                   for approval
                   for love
           I'm not sure I was able
              to give him
        what he needed then,
           before the letters demanding money

                  before the bank called daily
                  before mortgages and sports fees
          Now—now I know
              that regardless of what he needed,
                      all he ever got
                                was me.

The doorbell beacons again,
              my brother's family moved out west,
              my wife and kid are out,
                    a party with his team mates
                    he didn't want me there,
                              and I know why.

The incessant doorbell—
            a witch and a doctor
            candy dropped into pillow cases
            watching parents eye my cast
            and smile knowingly
                  thinking—he's home because of his leg
    They don't know—what they don't know.

My leg throbs   —the break reminding me that it was my fault,
                despite the paperwork I filed
                despite workman's comp
                despite the desperate words
            —there is no mistaking what the throbbing says
    Your fault—your fault—all your fault.
        and it's true,
             I caused it all:
                    the calls from the bank
                    letters requesting money
                                money that I didn't have
                                money my family needed
            That is when it started—
                    when I started drinking
to forget—to put a warm wrapping

The doorbell—a mummy, a princess, and a cartoon dog

        a warm wrapping around the mistakes
       quiet the blaming voice
    that echoes through my head
        you are not enough.
        I never was enough for them
         they are—
they are all so much better
      and so I put my costume on every day,
        and when it doesn't fit,
        when the seams are burst
        or the mask is missing
     I fill the voids with the warm oaken embrace,
   and I numb the pain.

The broken parts throb again,
  Your fault—your fault—all your fault.
     and I lean on my crutches the harder for it
       because I can't take the pain
        I can't see the regret
         the worry
         the dull ache
      and not try to silence it, fix it, like I did the car
         and the house
         and the mortgage
         and the—
       but not the marriage
  Your fault—your fault—all your fault
     and now the little white pills
         that take the pain away
      so I can feel
Normal again
Numb again
   like when I used to fix things—always things—

       I can fix this too
      fix the drinking,
a glass filled with amber liquid sits beside the orange pill bottle
          once I get past the pain in my leg
          once I get past the pain in my leg
          once I get past the pain
              and back to how things were
      before the bills piled up
      and the mortgage was due
      and the debt collectors called me
              at home
              at work
              at the bar
   so I will take my medicine and wash it down with self loathing,
        and I will fix this too
            just as soon as—

November

Another Round

Ping. A picture of two young kids smiling #tbt
        I try to remember if we have those pictures,
                my cousin and I,
      so I can post one too and remind people
                        that I am just like them,
                        and I was once a kid
                                    happy—
carefree.
But I'm not home yet,
                and who knows what waits—who waits
behind the bright red door,
                    and I have homework to finish
            Bring those grades up young man—my mother
            What are you stupid?—guess who.
Ping. A kid smiling in a little pool #tbt
      How do they have all these pictures
            who kept them stored safe in little boxes
                secured to bring out on a random Thursday in November
The car is out, the tv throws blue shadows
                              across the wall
                              in the living room
                              where he will be sitting
                              imperial in his infirmity
      as we are expected to do his bidding and take his wrath.
Ping. A picture of a father with his daughter on his shoulders. #tbt
Avoid, sneak, subterfuge, and stealth
            I fix a plate,
      no need to wake the sleeping bear
                who drank his honey,
      let him sleep it off, safer that way.
            On the books, the plate and sandwich teeter

                    and in slow motion
        topple to the ground, followed by math and science,
                        and I catch my phone before it too falls
            shattering the screen that would not be replaced.
But it is too late now,
                the rumbling growl of the bear
                the breaking surf
                the thundering, punishing winds
        wash over me as I stand there waiting for the hail.
His fingers,
            pushed into my arm,
                            usher me back
                                            toward the kitchen
but thinking better, pulls me to the scene
                            of the crime
                that woke the thunder from its repose
        the rest of my books fall, homework torn and pages smeared
                                            with mustard
                and to the kitchen again,
                            I stumble,
                                        to clean it up.
                the broken shards of the plate,
                        white against the pale blue carpet
                    misted with yellowed and torn bread,
        and I see the orange bottle, sitting on the counter, lid discarded
                                    the date on the side
                                    refill is still two weeks away,
                                        just before
Thanksgiving—
                        and for a moment I wonder
                how he is managing his pain
                                and remembering the bottle
                                            I try to forget.

Breaking Bread

"See, I promised I'd take you out to eat."
    Rewarded by the smile,
        alight in my soul the twin joys
        of love and respect
    specters of my life
        seen through the edges of her laugh
        lilting under the curtain of canned music
            "Only took a month" she chides
    her laugh could cure my ills
    infect me with a will to be more
"Could've been worse"
    I smile into her eyes
        eyes that make it easy
        to forget the bruises
        blooming beneath my shirt
"I could make you pay."
    Flushing because that sounds foreign
        when said with a laugh
        echoing words I hear
        in bellows
"But I wouldn't"
    Quick to adjust and readjust
        "I know,"
    her voice, a soothing balm
        on my scorched
        and battered life
            "That's one of the things I love about you,"
    How does sitting here make everything right.
        "how considerate you are."
    If I could live in her presence
        the blissful glow

       of her smile
       or the way her lips curve
       down when she concentrates
            "What's wrong? You're quiet."
"Nothing,"
    that is not nothing,
        but how would I tell her
        that my father is addicted
        drunk and abusive
she found a bruise the other day
        I flinched when we were fooling around
        and she pulled up my shirt
        to find the angry sweltering
        of fading lilacs in full bloom
           "Your dad?"
Reading me like a book
        I am thrown open before her
        and on my helpless pages
        she can somehow read
        what I need to say
without making me say it
           "You know you should tell someone."
the unhelpful advice of those
        helpful people who do not know
        what the maelstrom truly is
Thankfully the food arrives and we eat
        in a companionable silence
        that once held something more
        than what people can see
So we eat the ineffable silence
        breaking bread with no ulterior motive
        except to avoid the awkward conversation
        about abuse and love and hate
        all things as foreign to Joy as
        finding the words you don't want to say
because they will break the spell

and the goddess beside you will disappear into smoke
while the flames of your burning life consume you.
So instead you chew thoughtfully and break inside.

Focal Points

Put away the phone
            turn it off
     shut it out
Focus
                Focus
     Another message
     Another email
     Another homework
               not turned in
     Another storm
               on the horizon
I need to focus
I need to shift
         my lens
Focus
               on what is important
               in all the noise
     the assignments
     the notifications
     the problems
           at home
     the relationships
           at school
Focus
     before I'm over whelmed
     before the waves crash
         and I'm washed out to sea
         without a vest
         without a boat
         without a chance.
     before things go too far

                        a problem
                        too late

                        Focus
on what matters.
                        What matters?
        to me
        to my mother
        to my fa—teachers
                        assignments
                matters—matter
                        problems
                math—life
                        lenses
                experiments—perspectives
But now I'm so far from
        the sun—son
        success
        light
                        and I don't know
how to come back from the hole
                        I've dug myself
where all my lenses
        are dirt
        and scratched
        and refuse to refract
the view from
                        the back
never changes.

Colors

Sitting in my room
        scrolling
        through
        other
        people's
        pictures
Other lives presented on a screen
    flat and filtered against
    this pale dichromatic life
        people
        sitting
        at a table
        covered
        in food.
I remember the color of a Thanksgiving dinner
    brown turkey leaking juices on the plate
    red sweet potatoes hot under brown sugar blankets
    orange carrots drenched in butter
    crisp beans mixed with almonds
        people
        laughing
        and smiling
        and loving
        and sharing.
cornucopia of laughter and family
when those concepts mattered
the smells of food invited me to the table
knowing that I would find happiness there
where not there is nothing
except waiting ridicule reminders of my own failings
        perfectly
        arranged

> *plates*
> *of lovingly*
> *cooked*
> *food*

    brown liquid in his glass
    red hot anger, spewing venomous
    orange bruises under clothes
    sickly silence mixed with unease
I almost wish my life was as dichromatic as if feels

> *colorful*
> *pictures*
> *of families*
> *playing*
> *football*
> *on green*
> *lawns*

Instead the colors brighten and I need to cover my eyes
keep my head down and when my mother calls me down
to eat the food she slaved over to please him—
I will eat what they give me, digest the new normal
of a thankless-giving in this dichromatic house.

But Now in the Silence

The room never smells any different—indifferent to the time or day
The earthy smell of sweat and work and hope and wins and losses
        but now in the silence
        without the commotion of a team
        searching for the wins and losses
        measuring their meanings against
        past success and future battles
        to define their lives—
            deafening my life
            stretched out around me
The unbroken chain of pictures around the outer wall
People who started their lives in this room—like my grandad—my father
        but not me
Stare down from their pictures and judge as I stand emptying my locker
of the trappings that once held me as a member of my team—my family
        no longer mine
        the uniform taken, not tuned in
        ripped from the safety of my brothers
        and standing naked in my clothes
        before the sepulcher of my forgotten promise
        to be productive—
            I can't help
            rediscover forgotten myths
Remembering what I once told someone who is no longer the man he was
that I would play the game with honor when that word had meaning
        about heroes that never fail
and when the hope for another day, another game, another quarter
was enough to sustain me in the face of a world that no longer cared
        to face the adversity head on
        but standing now in front of my empty locker
        in the room that held so many of my victories

my ultimate defeat stares me in the face
and I sit, holding my cleats that seem too heavy
a burden to carry—

It's Whatever

"Dude they kicked you off?"

        Yeah, said I was too aggressive
            They don't know what aggressive is

"How'd the old man take it?"

        Screw him,
           He hit me
        I don't care what he thinks.
           and it hurt
           on more levels than he knows
        It's not like he drags himself to the games.
        I think the last time he saw me
           He doesn't even know who I am
        was when we played in middle school.

"Still, tough break.
Are you going to fight it?"

        It's whatever.
           I have no fight left
           If you only knew what you can't see
           Because I won't let you
        I was kinda over it anyway.
           Who needs people helping you
           realize that you're not worthless
           when the rest of the world sees
           the you they want to

"Really, I thought you loved it?"

        It's whatever, you know.
           whatever I want is taken away
           because the world decided
           love is a broken thing
           that only survives for fools
           and children

                                        Let's go out.

"Can't, I have homework."

                                        Come on, homework will be there tomorrow,
> *there's no real point in doing it*
> *time-sucks to fill the empty hours*
> *when avoidance works so much better*

                                        Let's live a little today.

"I promised my folk's
I'd make honor roll."

                                        What's one day?
> *I used to go for promises and honor*
> *but when they lose their meaning*
> *as all things will when you see*
> *the world for the bleak confines*
> *and dusty rooms it really is*

                                        What's the worst that can happen
                                        you miss a couple of assignments

"Sorry, man.
A promise is a promise."

                                        It's whatever.
> *not like I really needed—whatever*

December

Liquid Freedom

The smell hit me in the back of the throat
        constricting
        harsh
        forbidden
    and that—
        that hidden remedy
      to so many of my dad's problems
    The honey colored liquid
                that burnt going down
                that was hidden
                    in the back of the cabinet
                    behind the wheat thins
                that I had seen him replace
                        when he thought he was alone
                        and his tears subsided

I pour it into a glass
        from the cabinet
            to do it right
        and take a gulp

    My throat lashes out
            against the liquid flames
                that sears my senses
                and takes the breath
    I cough,
        cough again
                and again
my eyes water like his eyes
        unlike his eyes
      and I know that he does not feel
what I feel

                                        when he drinks
                    but for a moment
                            a breath's edge
            I pretend that his tears are something—
                        something other
                                than the signs of a broken man
                                    teetering on the edge of a glass
        Another sip, tentative this time,
                        one cough no fire
                        warmth floods my stomach
                                as the cool flames spread
            heating my face, and I can forget
            that yesterday was my birthday
                        and my mother,
                                    too tired
                                sore
                                            to bake a cake
                    cried because she didn't have anything to give me
        and my father
                        true to form
                                    didn't understand
                and met her rain with hail.

But I can forget that
                        here in this kitchen
                where we once had a home
                                a family
            while the fire water—an apt name—
coats my palate again,
            I cringe at the feeling,
                my tongue curling in on itself,
            and refilling the glass,
                            the bottle heavier
                                            for the loss of liquid,
                        I climb
                                unsteady

                                                            on the chair
                        to replace my father's bottle
                            knowing I will never need to hide
                                        what I am doing
                                because they are blind to my life
            and while my phone buzzes absently on the counter
                                        surely someone
                                                        momentarily self-aware
                                trying to fill the empty places in themselves
                                            with meaningless hashtags and hearts
But in this fog of smokey amber gold
                        I have no empty places
                    a sip opens up my senses
                        and at once
                                    fillets me and blankets me
                        and I am free from the need—
        —need to prove myself
        —need to be accepted
        —need to be noticed
        —needless
                    as the needles of heat spring from the glass and impale me
                            on the flaming sword of my salvation.
The second glass is empty and I think about a third,
                    but knowing my parents will be home soon,
                        I wash the glass and go to my room to bask
                                            in the fleeting freedom
                        the knowledge that the bottle un-bottles me
                so I can be free to not feel the world
                        locked away, I stare at the ceiling
                                        and wonder
                                    if this is how he feels.

The Party

Tucker's parents are away this weekend
        "So" she asks, but she know so, and why, and who
So, he's throwing a party—
it's not a four letter word you know
        "Drinking?" *drinking drinking drinking she always focuses*
                      on that one thing
                      on the one thing that calms
                      controls
                                  the roil of emotions
Yes, drinking, Joy
Drinking you don't have to do
        "But you—" *me yes me*
Of course I'll have some
                I'm not a liar
                no need to hide
                not my father
                              with his problems
                              his solutions to the world
                      I can control it
                          enjoy it
There's no reason I shouldn't
        "I'm good." *good—too good* "Let's go out to eat,
        I'll pay."
There'll be food there
                She never wants to go anymore
                      always trying to keep me from them
                from my fiends
                          the ones who found me
                          after the world turned its back
                          and I was thrown out
                                of the eden fields

            where cleats and nets define
                confine
      Locked in the world of Joy
        where she can sensor sense
          proffer purpose
You never want to go anywhere anymore.
  "That's not fair—not true" *true enough when I suggest it*
  I want to go eat—with you—not your friends.
  The you that helped me with my books
  and comforted me when everyone else—"
      That still hurts her and I see the kink in Joy's armor
        a little twist and she will break
            open her secrets
         and fold to my will
          my plans become her plans
     because I was the one that was there
       and I am still here
"Never-mind, I just don't want to go." *Joy looks down,*
    untouched trays of food between us
      because who wants to eat
           the forced nutrition
         when the good intentions
          create a broken chain
   so when we grab at the remaining shreds
      what was tears and we fall
Afraid what people will say
    The world according to Joy
      is defined by the hashtags
        of false faces in the new town callers
  "You're an ass—" *toothless venom*
Prove me wrong, *because it is what I want you to do,*
and come to the party.
  "Only if you don't—"
Don't put limits on me
    The world is too full of limiters
    dulling the speeds of youth

            with false expectations
           delivered with laser promises
          breaking the syllables of silence
       because ultimately they fear the power
           of unbridled youth
  Joy shakes her head and looks at the clock
  "Lunch is almost over,"
      This fact used to make her sad.
So you'll come?
    "Do I have a choice?"
Not if you want to spend time with me.
    I win. Last minute shot on the net from half field
      when time is short and you know you are right
        because the person you're talking to
         knows going is best but doesn't
           want to admit they're wrong
    because admitting is the same as losing
      and no one wants to take a beating.

Aftermath

Joy sat crying on my front porch
                       devastation raining down her face
    and I didn't know why.

        Her words gasped to her lips
then died like the fall of leaves in autumn
                but her face was not the peace of changing seasons
    instead her lips quivered like a quaking sands after an earthquake
she rung her hands around her phone,
                          my only clue

        like a child
        standing
        in a war-torn field
        grasping
        a frayed teddy bear
And she pulled away when I tried to comfort her
                            my hand, my touch
        once a balm to the searing wounds
                      of cruel words
        now seemed to burn her flesh so she needed
                  to pull away.
    Joy, I'm here for you. Let me comfort you.
        from the cruel bombs that our peers or neighbors
                carelessly throw over the fence
                        to disturb the patiently greening grass.
"How," voice quivered like lion cub in the jaws of a hyena, "how could you?"
    What, what did I do?
                she shakes her head
                        no.
    Tell me what I did so I can fix this.
"This isn't something you can fix."

                she opens her hands,
                      and unlocks her screen.
     85 new notices. An app, A picture.

                    I'm at the party, there was a lot of drinking
                    and she came onto me, Tia,
                            beautiful, popular Tia came onto me
                And what is a boy to do, I responded in kind
                    no harm in flirting
                                  with disaster
                                  with her
                because I love Joy, and everyone knows.

"Everyone knows," the quiver came before the rain
                        silently falling in a golden cloud

          She hands me another drink, my fourth
                fifth, there's no way to really tell
                      and I drink it, because not drinking
      would be rude, and I don't want to be rude.
              to Tia, beautiful, popular, Tia
                    and she leans in, to whisper in my ear

It's not a big deal but to her it clearly is *she's telling me something,*
    it was loud. It was loud, but I remember her words.

      Come with me, her skin was soft
            and her breath smelled like Bacardi.
                  She led me upstairs, to Tucker's parent's room
     I didn't want to be rude, not following her would be rude
            and I didn't want to
                        miss the opportunity
                    be rude to Tia
          I didn't think we were seen—we'd be caught

"There are others," it's an accusation, "how could you?"

Look, it's no big deal, I was drunk.
　　　　　　　It's clearly not my fault.
　　　　　　　　　She came onto me—I didn't want to embarrass her.
"I thought you liked me?" Her words fall like echoes of a forgotten bomb
　　　　　　　　dropped from the edge of the atmosphere
　　　　　　　　　　and they fall, falling

　　　　　　　Trevor's brother must have come in
　　　　　　　　　It was only a second—a moment
　　　　　　　　　　　she leaned in and I didn't want to be rude
　　　　Pulling away would be rude and she'd be embarrassed
　　　　　　　so I let her velvet lips which tasted like strawberry
　　　　　　　　　brush against mine—pulling away would be rude.

　　It didn't mean anything clearly she could see this
"You left me alone" for a moment "for an hour"
　　It didn't mean—
"It means something to me."
　　　　　　　and the echoes begin to fall
　　　　　　　　　from the stratosphere
　　　　　　　aimed at a spot
　　　　　　　　　　　no bigger than my fist
　　　And when she stood without looking
　　　　　　the casement struck
　　　　　　　　　　　and I knew that eden was destroyed.
"Good bye."

　　　　　　　I had looked for Joy at the party
　　　　　　　　　once I came back down—a moment
　　　　　　　　　　　but she had already left without me
　　　　　　So Tia got me another drink, fifth or seventh
　　　　　　　　　the world had slipped it's footings by then
　　　　　　　　　　　　and I could still taste the strawberries

　　Joy come back, it's not what it looks like—I just—Joy—Joy!
I hear it was silent

in the streets
                right after the bombs fell.

Betrayal

How could you, how could you, howcouldyou
You're supposed to be my friend
              You're supposed to have my back, bro
        Not supposed to attack when I'm down
I trusted you confided and now
              surprise I'm derided
When you could have kept your fucking mouth shut bro.
        But no, you need fodder for your feed
              check out my story
            the sordid—the gory details
Played out for the crowd
        well not ain't your parents proud.
You did me a real solid there
              let's air out all the dirt
        who gives a fuck
        who you hurt as long as people like it
            share it, comment, hashtag, react
'cause for that moment, though you stabbed me in the back
              you were seen.
It's obscene that you were willing to sell me out
            after all these years
        for a repost when the most you're gonna get
            is two minutes in the spotlight
before they riposte and forget, move on to the next
        because there's always more
another freak starting to peak
              But what you did goes down in history
Bro, no more now I know what you're for
                You know how I felt about Joy
        You knew and yet you blew any chance I had
because you needed to be next on the list—well fuck it and fuck you.

Don't go trying to blame me either bro
              she never would have known
        until you had to go and post it on your phone.

Darkness

Whatever, yeah, it's whatever
and the ceiling of my room, closed in as it is,
      moves ever closer, pressing on my chest
until I can't move, dangled over this gaping hole that is my future
carved from the softest sections of tomorrows failures,
and so it's whatever.

     I can hear them yelling downstairs, the storm is breaking
waves against the cliffs.
          We were supposed to decorate the tree tonight
     but I pretended to be sick
              of my failures
          of theirs
so that I could spend time up here and lay down
          down in the hole that I've dug myself.

     Grades are tanked
     off the team
     friends are losers
     and Joy left me
          the phone on my nightstand buzzes
   but moving my hand takes too much
             energy
             initiative
                        and I'm sure
I don't want to know who it is.

Down stairs—glass breaks and a door slams
     The rumble of his engine
              let me know
       the storm has moved on,

and I can still hear the rains softly falling,
        but who am I to try and help
   when I'm the mess I am.
So yeah, it's whatever
       because there is no real point
   in trying to stop the rain
         just because the storm has passed,
and although I know no spring will make the rain worthwhile
     I'll let it fall because stopping it
   would require finding a place
         that doesn't feel empty
   and full,
dislodged
       and crushed,
   simultaneously creating a storm in me
     that is my own fault
         and yet I deserve it
       because there is no other way I could be.

Ashes of a Fallen Star

Sitting in the woods, the wet log soaking through my pants
      is something I used to care about
            I used to care about a lot
      but wreathed in smoke,
                even the bite of the December night
    have no hold here because here is where the clouds dance.

      Puff and pass

    tomorrow I have to go to my grandparent's tomorrow
        I used to care about those things
      but I'll crack another beer instead
              because the night it cold and the beer is warm
    and the smoke it pleasant in my head
letting me float above the hollow places and not feel.

      Puff and pass

      I used to cate about what they thought
      My parents don't even know I'm gone
            I was in bed, not feeling well
    and I know they won't check on me tonight
because the storm came again tonight
    not like when I used to matter.

      Puff and pass

    We put the pills in a bowl in the middle
            we all brought our share
    my father should know his are gone
but that's not how things work in his world

where he knew I didn't know about his problems
I used to think he was a good man

Puff and pass

I take a couple and wash them down
and the beer tastes like piss
but the bliss of the smoke fills my empty places
it's the danger I am looking for to feel something
I used to feel something
and the bite of the air can never break my buzz.

Puff and pass

My head swims in the oblivion of ignorance
insolent to the reality of a world
to a world I once found so alluring
I used to see a tomorrow with the sun
only now the ashes of the fallen star
show me little more than dust.

Puff and pass

And even if that dust used to burn and light the sky
it is only something I know is true on paper
I used to know what truth was
because when the fire dies, and ashes fall
those that don't burn down to nothing
will never find their luster again.

January

Used to Be

They called me again yesterday,
    my used-to-be-brothers
        used-to-be-teammates
        used-to-be-friends
and said they wanted to hang again
          that I was not who they remembered
          that I was missing out on the fun
          that I was making a mistake
and I told them that I didn't need their pity
            because it was their pity
    they were giving me, not their brotherhood
              because that is broken, irrespirable
And I know that when a thing is lost,
          when the fish jumps the hook,
          when the play goes bad,
          when the storm comes,
      it is always best to let go
    and keep your hear downs
              because there is no reason to hold on
        when the ship is sinking around you
      and your lines have snapped.
There is no use moaning over
          what used to be
    when there is only what is.
        No point in seeing what could be
           if what used to be was
                because what was and will be
are incomparable with the is that is.

A Mother's Love

She wants to help, feels like she needs to,
        like the lie of our family needs to be kept in me.
I know what she thinks I see when I look in the mirror,
        but she doesn't know what I see when I look in the window
        standing outside in the cold winter winds
        looking at the warm light, the fire in the hearth
        burning like a fury fighting fate.
The flames cannot stave off the coming frost
        and like a frost that creeps over summer's growth
        paling the lushness of raw emotion—raw feelings
        the frost creeps even to the edge of those flames
        and they look to the heat as an exploded mythology.
Yet she tends the flames, putting wood in the hearth
        watching it crackle as it is consumed
        and all the while the frost bites at her heels
        and the fire, too hot in its effort to fight back the frost
        melts the toes of her shoes.
She thinks she knows what I see when I look in the mirror
        but she doesn't see what I see when I look at her.

Needs

I gave my Calloway driver away last week,
the kids next door outgrew his
and I couldn't see my dad golfing any time soon.
Yesterday I brought in some games my friend had wanted
we used to play them when he'd come over
but I haven't used them in a while.

I need to call my grandmother, and apologize
it'll make mom happy, because I didn't go last week
when the family was supposed to, it was just too much.
I said goodbye to all my teachers and my old coach
Friday, yesterday, and they all smiled kindly
but their minds were on the weekend and their own lives.

I can't blame them for that, it's not their fault,
not my parents either, but some things,
some people, just can't be helped.
My cousin's not around, off in college
and too busy to be bothered
I texted him an hour ago, but—

I think I'll bring my fishing pole into school
A kid in my fifth period class said he liked fishing,
and the last time I used it I caught nothing.
Maybe he'll have better luck than me,
maybe his father won't give up on him
like mine did before he found something new.

That just leaves my bike, I'm not sure who needs it,
who would want it, but I know that it won't be missed
in the garage where it always seems to scratch the car.

Maybe I'll just leave it at school, unfettered,
and it will find a new rider, a new home,
that will—will what? Need it more than me?
I tried to find Joy, talk to her, apologize
but she has avoided me since that party
when I made the fatal mistake and drove Joy away.
It is not her fault that I don't need it anymore—
better calling it an it, seems less valuable without naming
as if obscurity can dull the act that naming empowers.

Everyone thanked me for what I gave,
but never asked why I didn't need it anymore.

Sleep

I'm tired now,
                and soon I will not be—
the problem that I found in the mirror
                behind
    when I was looking for salvation.
                    It's funny,
    when you think of it
that the problems that we make
                      for ourselves
are not the problems that we imagine
          but instead their insidious claws dredge our hopes
     pulling them from the roots
and depositing them on the shore to rot
                while the flies buzz around.

    There is a floating sensation, and I want to close my eyes,
because they don't need to see the ceiling on my bedroom
             or the note on my dresser
or the empty bottle on the bed beside me
                    with my father's name printed on it.
    I had been holding it, I think, but it's just so hard
                  to get my fingers to move.
Laying down is so much easier, letting it go,
         my chest is heavy,
like when my cousin would sit on me as a kid
      when I took his stuff, and he wanted it back
              and after—but there is no after now.

My eyes can't stay open,
    and I feel like I'm suffocating
                      I want to gulp for air but

        it's so much work, and I'm tired of it
            of supplicating to the world
    pretending that their taunts don't hurt
          and that they can't see
through my broken home
     and my broken hope
            and my broken life,
  and my—my—broken thoughts.

I left the note for them to know—
              it was—
     not
                  their fault.
That I was broken before they shattered
     and the cracks—
          so long unseen
               revealed themselves to blind eyes—
while no one was looking,
     my mirror—
no longer cared—
   to hold the secret.

After all—
    it is really—
just a matter—of—

Unanswered

Knocking on the door to his room,
    he's been going through some hard times
transitioning
    in his cocoon, my butterfly emerging
can be hard for some people.
        unanswered knocking
    He's always been sensitive, my little man
But I know that he'll get through this
    when he was a baby, I remember his nightly cries
    and I would come into his room
        knocking
because I know he's stronger than he thinks,
    and I would hold him, rocking back and forth
    until he stopped crying because he was my little man.
and I will always be there to help him, even if his father—
    His smile would light up the room
    and his energy—
        unanswered
His father—they used to be so close before the money problems—
before the drinking—before the injury—the meds.
    It was like he was overloading with energy
    and even when he did wrong, and there were times—
I know I can't be a father to him, but I will always stand by him
and if I have to take a bruise to keep it from him—his father is a good man.
        troubled by the silence
    He would climb everything, yell sometimes, as kids do
    and when I would scold him, his smile and his energy
        Infectious
    I just had to laugh. There was never a straight face around him
    just ear to ear joy and love. My little inchworm—now in his cocoon
    a chrysalis waiting to sprout his wings and fly

I reach for the knob, turn it, but nothing moves
                silence on the other side
Nothing moves on the other side, the silence of a tomb
                danger screams in silence
        He was so excited when his dad taught him to fish
        they planned their weekend for a month, it was all he talked about
                Unanswered knocking
My heart beats hard, memories flashing through
        He was sick just before they went
        laying in bed, and sleeping.
                Knock harder
        and he was so worried that they wouldn't be able to go
        so we prayed together, I brought him soup, we cuddled
How do I unlock the door? I scream his name
                Unanswered calls
but the door doesn't move. I run my shoulder into it
                Unmovable moments
and for a minute the world stands still as the door shakes
        He came back from that trip so sunburnt
        that he looked like a lobster, but his energy never failed
        he literally bounced when he told me about the fish they caught
but it doesn't open. Banging on the door with both fists, I call again,
and my voice cracks as the rain begins, my fists like thunder on to door.
        His first bike, it was blue with some cartoon character on it
        he was afraid of the training wheels,
        but within a week, he was unstoppable
                Unanswered moments
        riding up and down the driveway until dinner
        speeding to the table, sweaty and smiling
I back up to the other edge of the hall,
                Unnerving silence
and run at the door, my slight frame against the wood
                Unanswered calls
and it cracks beneath my weight, and the world shatters with it
        I hold my son when he broke his arm
        I hold his hand when he got his stitches

> *I hold the bucket when he threw up*
> *I hold the line when he's in danger*
>> Unanswered questions

because a mother should never have to find her baby
> *My little inchworm, my butterfly, my little man*

laying on his bed, with foam on his lips, an empty pill bottle on his floor.
A mother should not have to wonder where things went wrong
and why her child wouldn't talk to her
> *I used to hold his hand as we crossed the street.*

The ambulance was quick but too slow for her heart
as it broke on the floor beside him and the empty bottle,
but I held his hand in the ambulance,
despite the tubes, despite the frantic work
> *he would look up at me and tell me*
> *"You're the best mommy ever,"*
> *and my heart would melt*

Now my heart breaks with each passing moment
and I wonder why—wonder what I could have done—
wonder what I did— and I know that my questions-
the questions that would sooth my soul and shatter me—
those questions will never be asked—
>> Always unanswered.

Numb

I left work when she called me—her voice barely audible
    "We're in the hospital—"
I was numb.
    "Bottle of pills—"
I was angry.

> *"Daddy," he'd come in when I was working*
> *in the garage, on the car,*
> *and he wouldn't leave me alone.*
> *He would bounce there and ask to help,*
> *his tiny hands holding the large wrench.*

I clock out of work and go to the car,
putting my tools in the trunk. The paper bag,
brown and unmarked, sings its song of oblivion
and I want to answer it because I want
to be numb again.

> *He grew up quickly, soon able to understand*
> *how things work—smart—and find the flaws*
> *the broken parts, where things were worn*
> *and we would fix them together, just us*
> *against the revenges of time.*

The weight was comforting in my hand
and the parking lot was empty.
Unstop the bottle and drink it down
brown warmth fills me with the comfort I need
the solace that I deserve because what he does is not my fault.

> *I taught him well, and he listened*

he mimicked what I did, what I said,
and I vowed to be better, for him, for them.
The garage became out place
where we could talk about the important things.

Empty the bottle. Put it back. Answer my phone.
    "He's awake—"
Take out my keys, the world shifts
    "He wants to see you—"
Smile because I cannot feel.

```
Not My Fault
```

I can see the way they look at me now,
        now that it's over
        now that I'm back
                from the brink of death
     the lightless brightness in the hooded dark of my subconscious
          They want me to talk about it,
    to explore why
        how
        who
    and I know they want to hear it was me
But this was not my fault.
        They don't really want to know—

—that when the coach kicked my off the team
        because I'm too aggressive
                too regressive, neanderthalic
    because I play to win and did what it took
                        what others couldn't do
        and someone got hurt. So he kicked me off.
Kicked me out of my family, my team.
        He took away what I loved, my right of passage
           my life.

—that when they wouldn't understand, couldn't help
            their assignments
            their expectations
            their judgements
    and because I couldn't live up to it
        their bar set too high for me
            unrealistic
                    and when I was drowning,

     my hand waving in the air for help
        they judged me for my emptiness
            because what is left when
   the gatekeepers of the future have hidden the keys.
     So I found the only open door
    to make myself disappear,
     hidden from their judgement
         and their expectations.

  —that when my phone would *Ping*. #same
    I would cringe inside because I know that *Ping*.
#betteryouthenme
       would be their silent judgment hidden
    behind their unambiguous anonymity. *Ping*. #selfie
         And my friends—friends who watch
      as the words beats me into submission
     friends who claim to care,
     but when you cry out for help
        in the only way you know how
    simply thank you for helping them get what they want. *Ping*.
#fake
     Because everyone is out for themselves,
       so why should one person matter? *Ping*. #lifegoals

  —that when I told her I was fine
    I never really meant it.
    And when I told him I didn't care
         about him
         or his drinking
         or his pills
      they were tearing me up.
    But despite the fact that they were supposed to—
to protect me
     all they ever saw was what they wanted
         I wanted
          to see

                                        to be seen.
            And so, despite the slow death that I gave them
                            every day, shutting down,
                    shutting myself away—giving up
                            they inclined to imagine everything
                                            was fine
                    when nothing really was.

—that the only person who is really to blame
            can never take the mantle
    because how can you be expected to live
                    with that kind of weight
            if—like Apollo and Icarus—the sun blinds you
                            melts the waxy armor
                    leaving you naked on the edge of eternity
    left to hold the mantle of your own failures
            while the world turns without you.

Choices

When you look into the eyes of the man you once loved
and see instead the eyes of a killer, who kills with inaction
there is something that dies inside, neglected, the flower cannot bloom.

> The drive from the hospital was silent. He drove
> carelessly fast, as if running from the memory
> of our son, laying in a bed, eyes closed, covered in tubes.

But I can never run from that memory because he runs,
into his bottles and booze and pills, and always away
from the people who should be his center.

> When we got our son settled in his room, he went down the hall
> into the kitchen, and I heard the chair move across the floor
> so he could get what I knew he hid to hide inside.

But I can never hide from the knowledge of what happened;
as much as I want to blame him, and his booze, and his pills
because the pills are what our son used on that judgement day.

> When I settled myself in bed and stared at the ceiling alone
> with my thoughts and the sound of a lonely glass on the kitchen table
> I know where the blame should be placed, I've made choices too.

February

Therapy

Cold winter winds blow snow around in little maelstroms
        outside the office window
and here I wait in a nondescript room,
        wait to talk to a nondescript man
        wait until it's my turn in the chair.
I don't want to be here waiting for someone I don't know
        to tell me how my problems are all
                my parent's fault
                in my head
                temporary
                beatable
because I took those pills in a moment of weakness
        and I know that I am not someone who runs
                from my problems
                like my father.

In this room, I am the victim, I am broken, I need to be fixed,
        but I don't want them to fix me because I am not broken.
            The world is broken, and the little man
                on the other side of the door can't fix the world.

            It's my turn—

We talk for an hour and I leave, while outside,
        in that nondescript room
        in that nondescript chair
        there is a nondescript person
        waiting for the little man behind the desk
        to fix the world.

Expectations

The bed shifted as she sat down,
                         her hand resting restive on my leg
I kept my back turned to the door
away from her sympathetic eyes
                       because who wants to face
                                the pain they cause other people
     The wind blew the sleet at my window
     little ticks in broken rhythms
I could hear her breathing
and squeezed my eyes shut
but I could still taste my tears
                       burning in the back of my throat
my jaw clenched, teeth grinding my weaknesses
     The house whistled as the winds shifted
     the sleet no longer pelting the window.
         sigh
Her voiceless disappointment in the me
spoke volumes that her voice couldn't utter
and as her sigh broke her rhythm
                     broke my resolve
warm tears slid silently from my clenched lids
and slit to sleep, with restless dreams, on my pillow.
Her voice, horse from—from her disappointment
              My baby boy—
her voice, the voice of pain, voice of my childhood
         I'm so
                  disappointed
sorry that I couldn't—
that I couldn't see the pain
that you were in, that was drowning
drowning my little man.

tears biting at my throat, clawing emotions
>*Because I made a promise to you*
>*when you laid in this room,*
>*played in this room,*
>*as my little baby boy,*
>*that no matter what else happened*
>*I would always—*

her voice cracked. Waves at the base of a lighthouse
threaten to tear the foundation of stone.
>and the wind whips handfuls to sleet
>sandblasting the images of past joys.
>>*always be there for you.*
>>*But I wasn't, was I.*
>>*You have been alone in this*
>>*because I have been—*
>>*been preoccupied with my own problems.*

Like when she steps between me and the gathering storm
>*That's not fair—*
>>Here come the excuses
>>reasons why I disappointed her
>>once again.
>*not fair to you*
>*my precious angel*
>*who thought the world too dark*
>*to see through the gathering storms*

The bed shifted a moment, shaken by the winds of past storms
>*and find a time when the clouds will part*
>*when the sun can once more shine—*
>*my son can rise once more.*

I press my eyelids against her truths
>which are not a reflection of my truth
>because if they were, if—
>>*I'm sorry that I wasn't aware enough—*
>>*good enough—strong enough*
>>*for you to know that I was there for you,*
>>*and when the weight became too much,*

> *when the world became too much*
> *I am here.*
> *Without judgement*
> *without scorn*
> *without fear*
> *because there is nothing in this world—*
> *nothing in you—that is too dark for me*
> *to walk beside you, through the darkness*
> *until we can find the light—together.*
> *There is nothing—*

Broken rhythms of her breathing
> *nothing—*

Stealing the metal of my resolve,
my shoulders hitch as the air fights the depths
that stream down my face from my burning eyes
> *I would not go through for you.*

Rolling on my back, I watch her shoulders shudder
in the silent emptiness of her own pain
and—
> *I'm sorry.*

She turns her tear streaked face to me,
looking down from red puffy eyes
> *I'm sorry.*

I sit up and hold onto her as we huddle together
clinging to the rocks while the waves crash,
unchecked, against us.

> The sounds of the sleet on the window fades
> to the patter of wet drops, heavy
> against the roof of the house where I live.

Coming Back

They want to make sure I'm
                                     comfortable
                                     ready to come back
         to the realities that drove me to
                 to do what they see as unthinkable
give up on everything.
         Truth—
Truth is that no, I'm not ready
                 not ready to see everyone
         their judgement in the silent eyes
but that doesn't matter
         because I need to come back
                 I need to face what I did
what I wanted to do
         and overcome it,
and I can't do that in a hospital,
         with sterilized walls
         and sterilized interactions
     so I'm coming back.

Work—Work—Work—Work

     in a separate room—
         a separate world—
       from my peers so I can catch up.
    and suddenly everyone cares
                             about me
                     and my feelings
                          about bullying
                   and lawsuits
because as much as they want to think

        they understand,
they never could know that what drove me to it
     what put the pills in my hand
              is unknowable
       and I don't even understand
     how I can come back from that dark hole.

Work—Work—Work—Work

Cordoned off from the world,
     another sterilized room
without the judging eyes,
        and every day we talk
    teachers—counselors—administrators
        and every day I do more work
   Math—Science—English—History
      and get more restless
because I want to come back to my life
           the life I tried to leave
    and escape these sterile rooms

Work—Class—Work—Work

    One break in the tedium.
One break in the sterility
     and I breath the air
before the class comes in
    the cacophony washing over
         the artificial beach of serenity
     and waves begin to erode,
        already,
   the carefully manicured coast of my mind
and I look at my desk to avoid their eyes
       and the judgement that I know is crashing around me.
    when I feel a hand pay my back,
        and another—another—another—

                    comforting words—words of welcome.
and I look up at smiling faces and encouragement
                                and for a moment I'm confused
        because this is not what I expected.

Work—Class—Work—Class—Work

                Transitioning—
        that's what they call it,
the incremental increase
                from what you were
                                to what you are
                        or what you are
                                to what you will be.
And I am eager now to come back
                back to my classes
                                my family
                my friends
                        my life
and discover what comes after the thing I can't really talk about
        because something must come after that
                the moment when, in my chrysalis
I ate my own poison—because I need to believe
                                that what I did made a difference for someone
                        that transition is transformation
                and while I don't know what I am
                        I might be able to find
                what I might become.

Work—Class—Class—Class—Work—Class

        Music—Science—English—History
Getting closer to where I was before,
                catching up—pushing through—coming back.
        Talking to people who know how I'm feeling
                        because they actually cared to listen,

and although I thought my voice echoed in the hollows,
    they had heard me even then.

Whispers

there are times that I can forget

         the whispers

that everyone knows
about my weakest moment
when the world came crashing down
and I broke under the weight of

         the whispers

my mistakes and my worries
broken Atlas fallen to his knees
before his tormentor

         the whispers

leaning on the pillars for support
and punished for his past
but for all his flaws and faults
he taught the people to see

         the whispers

their way through the darkest night
across the fathomless sea
with nothing more than

         the whispers

stars to guide them
and if I am a broken Atlas
weighted down by the world
propped on my shoulders
punished, tormented

         the whispers

I will, like Atlas, find relief
from my burden and discover

         the whispers

are not what I once thought.

Thunderheads

The day the storm broke
I saw the gather clouds
and retreated to the safety
of my room before the weather
unnaturally calm, could shift
but that didn't stop me from hearing
the thunder and the lightening
the fury and the rain
that never quite found the ground
because some storms rage
without releasing their full power
until the winds have picked up
enough to carry the moment.

But that day I saw the coming threats
and I knew where to hide
because the other storms were just a drill
and something about the color of the sky
told me that this would be different.

When you learn the signs of the storms
they become easier to predict
meteorology when the storms are outside
in the sky, and the color changes
are seen with your eyes
and temperatures with your skin.

But when you feel the color change
with your ears and see the temperature drop
with your eyes, you know
meteorology has nothing on the storms

that you are chasing or that chase you
because there is less concern
when you're only worried
about a damaged roof or broken tree,
and your neighbor doesn't walk out surprised
that the storm didn't take their house too.

It is strange when you hear the storm breaking
not opening up the sky to send rain skittering
and small creatures run to hide in their burrows;
when a storm breaks, and the thunderheads
have lost their towering crowns,
the silence that follows is something felt
more than heard because the sun,
hidden for too long, pushes through the rain
and takes its place in the sky to shine down
warm and bright into the gloom that stayed too long.

When I heard the rumble, the last peal of thunder,
I knew this time was different, and the silence
felt both darker and warmer that silences before.

The Terms of Your Surrender

There comes a time in everyone's life
                when they need to come to terms
                              with their own surrender.
    Looking in the mirror, my own disheveled reflection
        glaring in the glass
                      knowing that all you can ever see
        is your past self
      because even the speed of light is slower than time
                and there is a comfort in knowing that.

I know my mother is sitting down stairs
            at the kitchen table coming to terms
                        with the man that she married.
    Looking at each other, eyes that found no faults
        glaring at the glass
                knowing after this evening
        things will change
    because sometimes love is not enough to last
                and there is a comfort in knowing that.

My eyes are swollen and red from the tears
            I shed when she told me what had happened
                        with the man that she married.
    A splash of cold water on my face, rivulets on my cheeks
        looking on myself with softer eyes
                because healing can't start
        until forgiveness comes
    although forgiveness of your own shortcomings
            is sometimes harder to seek.

Her eye is swollen and bruised from last night

                                      she shed the timidity that held her back
                                                                                                    from doing what needed doing.
            A splash of warming whiskey in my father's glass
                      looking like he wants to cry
                                    because healing can't start
                    when no-one asks for forgiveness
           although forgiveness might not be possible anymore
                              some breaks don't heal.

Deep breaths to steady my nerves, and more water on my hair
                            to smooth things down and find a place
                                            where I feel in control of something.
            Working out the tangles can be therapeutic sometimes
                      because it is a form of change and control—
                            a small change,
                    sometimes, is enough to help you find your ground
        in an ever-shifting world where people aren't black and white
                          and some promises don't last.

Deep breaths to steady her nerves, and she begins to talk to him
                            to smooth things out, and find a place
                                        where the separation won't hurt.
            Working out the tangles before the papers are filed
                    because there is no coming back from where they are
                          a small change,
                  that has consequences beyond their current state
        in an ever-shifting world where people aren't good or bad
                            and some loves don't last.

These are the times in our lives, when the winter storms have passed
                            and the calm winds of an early spring
                                            kiss the delicate new growth.
            When the last words spoken are the only words to say
                    after all the words that never had the meaning of action
                          and meaningless actions
                            only had the power of words not spoken

These are the times in our lives, our loves, where you need to define the terms of your surrender

March

A New Normal

The human mind can get used to anything—
        that's what they told me at the hospital
                when I woke up, ashamed, from after day
        and I asked how I was going to look everyone in the eye
                after I let them see that I am weaker
than they are—than I want to be.

In time, you'll find a new normal—a better normal,
        and while I wanted—want—to believe them
                it is hard to think about while you're laying in a bed
in a hospital gown, with the tubes and the beeping,
                but I didn't know how much harder it would be
to believe the platitudes in the real world.

Normal doesn't even enter into my world right now:
        Avoid your phone, social media is corrosive, the internet lies
                but what they don't understand is that life happens
my world—the old world—is held together by likes and comments
                and even when it falls apart and drags you down
it feels better to be involved than alone.

They have their playbook,
        their proven methods of recovery that have worked for years
                I don't have years for it to work, I have now
        because tomorrow is coming whether I want it to or now
                and today is where I need to live, yesterday simply was
        I need a different playbook—my own new normal

At school, my peers and teachers look at me as fragile
        and most people will respect that
                but there are always those looking to exploit

    my weaknesses for their social gains
        and my actions—
                those I still can't put in words—
    become chum,
until their dark eyes glaze because there is blood in the water.

My gutted self-esteem lays exposed while the predators lurk,
    some days it's too hard to hold it in, hold them back,
        those are the days that are the easiest, and my erraticism
    excused because I am damaged, fragile, broken
        and only the most desperate or the sadistic
want to play with a broken toy.

And so I languish in the imposed exile of the doctors and my mother
    who do not understand that I cannot become whole,
        cannot fully heal, without a connection
    and the real connection, the normal world
        exists in social media and curated lives
and my forced asceticism can never be my new normal.

Talking It Out

We're sitting on the bench
        watching the empty soccer field
                      on what feels like
        the first warm day in forever.
"Dude," he breaks the silence, "where you at?"
        I'm here and I'm not, but he doesn't need to know that.
"No you're not," he leans back,
                always confident,
                always sure,
                      "You're somewhere else."
    Just enjoying the warm weather. It's been a while.
"Winter does that," he laughs
                always relaxed
                always smiling.
      We sit for a while,
                in silence,
                      in the sun,
    taking it in.

He breaks the silence
                always ready
                always curious
"Can I ask you something?"
        I guess. But I know
            by the way he asks
                    that I won't like the question
"I want to help," we've been friends since kindergarten
                    "but I don't know what to do."
      Like I do—
"Why'd you—I mean—you know?"
           Very articulate, but how do you articulate the un-statable?

  Unstable as I was, the question
        harmless in intent
    breaks the reverie of the moment and shatters
the calm of the warm sun
        sending chills down my spine
    and I wait for the words to come
  for the way to say the unsayable
       I was hopeless
         hurting
         broken
         angry
         devastated
       all of that and none of it
         numb to the emotions that flooded me
    drowning in the fathoms of feelings
      and yet
        while immersed
  utterly and unmistakably numb to the darkness and the light
"I'm sorry," he quickly retracts in my silence, "that was a dumb question."
  But it's not a dumb question,
        I watch a bee fumble on a dandelion
  because it's the same question I'm searching for an answer with.
"I guess I just wanted to say—" his voice sounds lost,
         so unlike himself,
"I guess I just wanted to say that I'm here dude
    —you know—if you need me."
  Thanks, I know. And I do know.
      Always helpful
      Always there
He leans his head back and looks at the blue sky;
  I watch the bee as it finds its wings,
    and together we sit in silence, and I know
It's good not to be alone.

Ordinary Day

Like any ordinary day
                            the alarm goes off at 6:00
snooze—five more minutes
       warm under my covers, not ready
                            to face another day,
today will be different
              different because today is tryouts,
       but those can wait—five more minutes.

English, science, history, gym, Lunch.
       I avoid her through the day,
                 I lost Joy before
          and I know there's no going back.
       She's nice to me, smiles in the hall,
                     but she doesn't want to talk.
       Math, then Music.

The homework is piled on,
       the sun is hidden behind the clouds
          a light rain pelts the diamond
                     and I don't care
because walking through the locker room is like coming home.
          This time I will
                      be better
                      be stronger
                      be calmer
                      not get kicked off
          because this time I have a chance
                    for something more
                    than living my family's life—my father's life
                          this time I'm finding my own way,

     and I know that I will find my place
       in this school—life—world.

"Dad moved out last week" *and the storms passed,*
        "but Mom's letting him come over tomorrow."
  I tell everyone who will listen,
    "We're going to get the car running again"
       we can fix things that time has broken
  "I've missed him the past few weeks."

   driving, swinging, putting, and drills.

     "My dad and I used to go driving,"
   there's something nice about not being known
       about not having expectations
        to live up to
    and finding your own way
      in the world.

"They said about half of us are getting cut," Mom looks concerned.
   "Don't worry. I'm sure I'll make it, and if not I'll be all right."
    She wants to trust me, I can tell,
       when you see your kid laying on the bed
      finding them the way she found me
        it has to be hard to believe
  that they will ever be all right again,
    but she tries.
"I'll know tomorrow—lunch time."
  her question is draped with worry.
    "I'll text you."

            Her phone rings
            and she picks it up
            but doesn't say much
            with her words,
            her face could never hide

                                                            emotions that crash like waves
                                                            and tear at the foundations
                                                            of the ragged emotions
                                                            from a woman grieving
                                                            a love that has not truly died.

   "Who was it?" I ask, shift the focus so she doesn't worry
                        about me, but the worry on her face
               is etched with a finality
                              and the tears that make her pull over
       scare me more than the empty look in her eyes.

   "I need to tell you something that is going to be hard to hear—"
                  her words are lost in the crashing waves of emotion
                        that can only follow the words
       no mother wants to tell her son.

   At home, I sit in the garage and cry alone among the unused oil rags.

Secrets

They don't need to know the reason
        why the car is not getting fixed
this week or next because they won't understand
        so I let them assume that he was busy—
                got distracted—
            didn't want to come—
    because those will hurt less than knowing
        that the car is not going to be fixed
because when time decides to exact its toll
        there is nothing we can do to shore up
    the fading walls of a life that was
        with the porous walls of future hopes.
So I will let them think that he's with a new girlfriend
        because they can understand that
    that would hurt me—
            —but this is worse
    because girlfriends are temporary
        distractions from a family
but when—when you forget to change the oil
        and the heat becomes more than you can take
            there are places that we can't come back from,
    and when some engines sputter,
        when some pistons seize,
    turns out that some engines
        can't be rebuilt.

A Mother's Lament

When the house is quiet late at night,
is when I feel it the most—the regret—
when mistake after mistake eats away at me.
Like a termite devouring the fibers of our home.
Our home—can you still call it a home
when all that's left are broken dreams
of a life that should have been better,
of a million little promises made and broken
each time one more fiber taken away
chewed up and succumbed into dust?

This poison, a warm amber in the light from the kitchen bulb,
multifarious monster hiding in a bottle, high on a shelf
but still ready to drag his world—our world—my world
to the ashes of self-pity. I should have been stronger for them both.
Watching the whiskey circle the drain, giving off its cloying smell
that he would come to bed with on the good nights—
the bad nights were filled with worry that his storming rage
would make some final mistake that I could hide with makeup.
But it wasn't this poison that got him in the end—another end.
The tears that are falling are not for him—not for the broken man
who found his own end in the same accident that he lived,
one, I'm sure, he'd have apologized for, the norm every morning
when makeup covered the damage from the storm the night before.

I cry for the one I could not protect, could not shelter
from the storm life put before him, the hail pings of social injustice.
Alone in the darkened room, tears stroking my cheeks,
I know that he is hurting and hiding, and I pray—
I pray that while life is horribly unfair to him,
he remembers—this time—that he doesn't have to be alone

that I'm here for him, that I'm strong enough for him
even if I wasn't what he needed before. I'm done with crying.
A mother's tears can make a child feel so small and helpless,
and I cannot—I will not put that on his already weighted back.

And so I sit here, salty stinging eyes
as the tears stiffen on my cheeks.
I know that I am all he has left,
and though I will never be enough,
I will be everything I know to be
and find the strength to be his windbreak.

Boys and Men

When I was younger,
        my father brought me fishing
    to a pond he knew
           where his father brought him
when he was younger.

        It's strange to think of your father
        when he was a child, innocent
        unsure of the world he's in
        because when a boy becomes a man
        he learns that there is no real difference
        between the boy that was
        and the man that is.

In the garage is the car
        that we were going to work on
    the one we used to fix
        that helped us to get where we're going
I know I don't know enough to fix it alone

        Sometimes when the oil would drip
        on the puddles in the driveway
        I would see the iridescent sheen
        and imagine that it was a portal
        to another world where boys could play
        and not worry about school or chores
        even then escape was absurd

In the kitchen I can hear my mother cry
        she doesn't know that I am listening
    and she won't know

                      because she wants to be stronger for me
so I will let her be what she needs to be.

        I don't remember when I realized
        that my parents weren't perfect
        their flaws are so much smaller than mine
        that they seem insignificant compared to me
        and their monumental presence
        can never be diminished by knowing
        that they are sometimes scared too.

In my room I sit and listen to the house
        as it settles into its own new normal
    of quiet nights and subtle days
            and I realize that nothing will return
to the way it was when I was the me before.

        I always through that change
        came with a warning, something loud
        but it turns out that change is not an explosion
        instead it is the slow wearing off of a veneer
        that takes the shine off of something new
        and replaces it with something less flashy
        yet still more comfortable, broken in.

I know I am all that she has left,
        and that she is afraid for me,
     but while I can't stop being scared,
           I can stop running from my fear
because boys run but men stand.

        It's the first thing that people learn to do
        on their own, without help, before we can even eat.
        We stand up, leaning on our parents for support.
        Even before we walk, we stand,
        and when we fall down, when he struggles,

there is always someone to help us up
and real men stand by those who helped them stand.

April

What is There to Say?

What is there to say
          for a man whose choices made him leave
    long before he finally left,
          and leaving, left broken pieces behind.
I don't—can't really place the blame on him
          but there is no one else that I can see
    who is responsible for his actions
          when his acts are so selfish and so final.
But someone needs to speak for the man
          who once showed me how to hold a wrench
    when the most complex thing to fix
          could be fixed with tools.
Now I'm sitting here without the tools I need
          trying to find the words to describe the life
    of a man who didn't keep his promises
          and learned to run without standing.
The blinking curser mocks my efforts
          to put my feelings into words
    because despite his shortcoming
          I still love the man he used to be
before he became the man he was
          before the storms broke the placid water of my childhood,
    scattering the iridescent sheen of youth
          leaving me without the words to say—

A Father's Song

It took a while to figure out
what to say for you today,
but I wanted to stand up here—
to stand for you,
for all the times
you stood for me.

                Memory is a funny thing;
                everything depends on the moment,
                like a picture of your life,
                and although I was only a moment
                at the end of your's, you were everything
                at the beginning of mine.

        My earliest memory of you
        is your smile, it was warm
        and safe and joyful,
        made me feel, even without knowing
        that I could trust you
        and you would protect me.

There are others too, pictures in my mind
like the time we got lost looking for a camping spot
and we had driven past it, just a few feet
only to walk around the whole lake,
some of you may be surprised to know he laughed it off then.

        I'm not going to sugarcoat my father's life
        he made a lot of mistakes, and there were times—
        times that don't need to be pictures
        ones I wish I could forget, but everyone knows

                the faults of an imperfect man.

                                What you might not know is: When I was ten
                                he brought me into the garage, it smelled bad
                                oil and gas and body odor and something else
                                that I didn't learn about until much later,
                                and showed me how to change the oil in a car.

We laughed a lot that day, he smiled a lot
and I ruined my new shirt—mom was pissed—
and it's funny that what I remember about that,
other than how to change the oil in the car,
is how the room smelled.

                                I don't know why it's the smells that get me
                                his aftershave, his work shirts,
                                this jacket that I'm swimming in,
                                and yes, his brand of whiskey, near the end—
                                now—that smell was all that was left.

            I'm sorry, we know where my father ended up
            we know his drinking and his oxy were his end
            and half of you are sitting there wondering how long
            until I'm in the pine box too.
            Those of you too squeamish to look at me know.

But what you don't know is the man
he was before your pictures of him
when I broke my arm and he read to me
the man who held my bike and taught me to ride
the man who loved my mother, before his storms.

                                I won't sit here and tell you he was perfect
                                there aren't enough filters in the world
                                to hide his blemishes, but I can tell you this—

        that when you stand before his casket
        to say goodbye, remember this:

The man who lays there, broken and defeated
was once the entirety of the world to his little boy
and even if he failed to keep his promises
to me—to my mother—if I can see his faults and forgive
what makes you so much better that you can't?

Breathless

     Hundreds of messages,
              texts and tweets,
    notifications and emails
from my teachers
       from my peers
   from stores I shop at
            and people I don't know
and they all want my attention
                            now.

    That's how it is for the modern teen
          know who you know you need to know
             need it **now**
    yesterday isn't quick enough any more
              and unplugging
        was never really an option
because then you are adrift
            and out of control.

    It's hard to focus
when my phone keeps beeping
      *Ping*ing the newest trend
   updates,
          reminders,
likes,
              homework,
     hangouts.

Everything is happening **now**
       everything at once
   without a break or a breath

       because to not engage
     is to be ostracized
  and when I get the *like*
         it's validation of my life
  because to live unvalidated is to live unseen
     and I want to be seen.

More than anything I want to be seen
   for who I am—
       who I really am,
    and not for the second skin I wear
wrapped in the illusion of self worth
      drinking the delusion
            spoon fed through a screen
   where my very definition
     is a negotiation for a *share*.

With all that, there is too much
   of *noticing* and *reminding* and *pinging* and *liking*
     because in all that noise, all that **now**
       there is another voice
     that lost its will to speak
  and another set of eyes
    that forgot how to see.

  So I will not unplug from the constant
     streaming of the content of my life
but I will try to take a break
     from the cult of **now**
  and my intimacy with immediacy
       will have to wait.

Breath—

Quiet the noise of **now**
     and live the world on my own terms,

       where I engage when and where I want
                not where I want to want,
because part of growing up,
         of the transition to—something more
                  is finding the will to control
     the moments that we live in because
as my father found out too late
             the moments are pictures
        fleeting into the background
   in the static of tomorrows and yesterdays
and the most important days
              the succession todays
       should not be filled with
    yesterday's regret
           and tomorrows worry.

Breath—

Mulligans

The flowers in the beds are blooming again
and that patch of lawn that died last year
when we had a bonfire to celebrate
my graduation from middle school
has started to grow back,
erasing reminders of past success.

The car isn't in the garage anymore
I couldn't fix it, I didn't know enough
so my mom had it towed to the shop
the oil-soaked rags have lost their allure
and the smell of gas and metal
don't hold happy moments anymore.

They say that spring is a good time
for starting over because everything is blooming,
but there are some things that the coming rains
can't wash clean, and some withered bushes
that couldn't survive the winters cold
need to be pulled up or pruned back.

My therapist says that I need to be like the trees
and shed the dying branches of past growths
that didn't survive the cruel winter's storms
to allow the sun to shine down on
the newer, fledgling sprouts that inevitably come;
He says the forest has a way of renewing itself.

I like the idea of pruning my past moments
letting them fall like clippings on the grass
and gathering them up, fine someplace

out of the way, someplace unneeded
to let nature break them down
until they too can fertilize the future.

So I stand looking in the mirror and talking
to myself about the past moments that didn't—
and I let my tears enumerate my past mistakes
clipping my sentences at where the line is healthy
thanking my mother and my luck that I am still here
to prune these unhealthy moments.

Like a golfer out for his first real round, I tee up
knowing that I'm going to miss the ball more often than not,
but in the end, my handicap will be my own
because when you swing for the hills and miss
it's good to know that there's a cushion
and sometimes you get to take a mulligan.

Apologies

I.
Hey Joy,
>I hate that I'm standing here
>in the cafeteria next to her friends
>where I do not belong asking for what I don't deserve
>>*What do you want?*
>
>Her voice brings me back to winter
>to the snows and the ice and the slipping
>but I have to continue—

How are you?
>It's lame, a lame start
>because there is no aborting
>no going back now that it's begun.
>>*Fine.*
>
>The word that never means what it says
>but in this case was probably true
>before she had to say it.

I'm just going to say this,
I screwed up—with you—
>>*You think?*

and I know
that there's no going back,
>because seasons keep moving
>and it's time for winter to end

and I know that you shouldn't forgive me,
I'm not even looking for forgiveness,
but I want to say I'm sorry
for the way I treated you
and for the things I said and did.
>Because it's not forgiveness
>that I need from you

  absolution is too high a cost
  and completely out of my control.
           And?

  And what did I expect?
  My shoes are caked in mud
  from yesterday's rain.
And I'm sorry.
   I walk away
   because apologies
   don't mean forgiveness.
   Her hand on my arm stops me
   the chill of regret passes through
   and I stand to listen

         Listen, I was rude just now
         but what you did hurt me
         and seeing you again doesn't help.

I know.
         I'm not done—
  Why does apologizing feel final?

         If you're really sorry,
         if you really want forgiveness,
         then don't do it again, to someone else
         because I'm sorry is an action not a word.
  A chilled wind blew through the open window
  winter's last gasps.

II.
There are so many things that I'm sorry for.
        and there are so many times
        that I know you were there
You tried everything,
you took the brunt of his storms
because you were trying
to protect me.
        —to save him
        to fine peace in a peace-less home
                You have nothing to apologize for,
                those were my choices, my burdens to bare
Maybe, but I didn't appreciate
        them—you
what you were doing
when you pushed me away
        from him
You were trying to save me
keep me from getting hurt.
                I'm sorry it didn't work.
        In a way she is right
        but not in the way she means
        because reality is not so cut and dry
                You got hurt anyway.
No, not really
not like I could have.
                But you didn't come out without scars.
Scars are places where we've been made stronger
He said that once, before the storms.

III.
    It's easy to forget the times before the dark clouds gather
    and the winter winds break up the leaves that withered on the branch.
        Dude, look out—to the left
    Focus back on the screen, back on the game
    that I gave him before I tried to run
    he returned it yesterday and asked to come by
    to play it like we used to.
        Nice shot.
Thanks.
    We picked up like nothing ever happened
    like a lie, that we both accept as truth.
        Wanna get something to eat after this round?
    But a lie is still a lie,
    even when it's the most comfortable thing in the room
Sure.
We got some wings in the freezer.
    and there are times when what doesn't need to be said
    still needs saying.
About before—
    What do you say to a friend you ignored
    pushed away when they tried to help
    and accused of trying to ruin your life.
        Don't worry man,
        everyone has their shit.
        Nice shot with that last guy,
        I think we're gonna beat it this time.
    It's funny how sometimes forgiveness
    comes before the apology.

IV.
I want to tell you something,
but you don't have to respond,
just listen. I need to say this.
       The sun shines down on my shoulders
       and I watch my shadow on the green grass.
       Birds sing happily on the branches of the trees
       who shift in the light breeze, stretching
       after the long winter slumber.
I wanted to say that I was sorry
for not realizing that you were—
I guess that you were as flawed as I am.
       I leaned my bike against one of those trees
       and I see it now, lonely, out of the corner of my eye.
       Taking the ratchet from my back pocket
       I spin it and listen as the gears click smoothly,
       ticking away the revolutions.
It's just I saw you as something else
something more than was fair to you
because I needed you to be something more.
       The rustling of something in the trees
       makes me look away—look up.
       The warm air fills my lungs
       and the smell of flowers, freshly bloomed
       makes me grin, despite—
That's not your fault—not your failing.
You don't need to apologize for it,
so please don't try. Just let me finish.
       A bee buzzes lazily through the air
       and lands on one of the flowers
       that I'd brought with me because it's—
       it's what people do in the movies
       when they come to talk.
Before—well before everything
you were the person I idolized—
wanted to be like, and just couldn't.

      The wight of the ratchet felt comforting
      in my hand as I fiddled with it
      letting the time click away in relative silence
      not wanting to leave
      but running out of things to say.

I'm sorry I pit that weight on you
that burden. I'm still mad at you though,
I think I have that right, but I'm sorry about that too.

      Reaching out, I place the ratchet on the stone
      and, making sure it won't fall, turn back to my bike
      leaning on the smooth bark of the birch tree
      that shades his grave. He said they were his favorites,
      because they always bent with the wind.

The Hatchling

Outside my window
                    high up in the tree
there is a bird's nest, with three small eggs
      I don't see them often, the mother bird
her charcoal wings tucked in and her rusty chest
              warming her eggs
        as the sun cuts its way through the branches.

I found it two weeks ago,
              when the chirping woke me up too early
      but it was nice to hear,
and wake up early isn't all that bad.

Every morning when I wake up,
              I check on the nest
there's something comforting   about knowing it's there
       tucked away in the branches of the tree
secure from the light spring rains and predators
             why exploit weaknesses
         for the joy of having power over someone else.

Most of the eggs have hatched now,
           but there is one, still in the shell
      the mother watches the egg, sits on it
and I'm afraid that she'll be disappointed.

Getting ready for school, I double check
                my homework done and packed
because I'm starting to like the feeling
      of being caught up, on time, successful.

Feeling confident that I'm ready for what comes my way
                for a change of pace
                      is something that I have often overlooked.

People smile at you more when you're not behind,
                they're proud of you—of me
           because other people like to see success
they want those around them to win.

Even my friends seem happier to be around
                      my real friends, who stuck it out
despite constantly pushing them away
           getting lost in the noise of life
as opposed to living it was exhausting
                    and it's good to breath
           for a change.

I look once more at the nest, backpack on my shoulder
                and the mother's moved aside
           watching the last baby break through its shell
and reach its neck up looking for food.

May

Here's the Trick

Listen up—
      Here's the trick—
            Take my advice—

Everyone has something to say
        their two cents to add
    often without listening first
           without knowing the score;
   last year that would have driven me crazy,
       last year in the time before—
             before everything.
Now though, now I know
    that their advice, their thoughts
          are just that—
        their thoughts. I don't need them
  and while they may be good
        and helpful
      thoughtful and kind,
           they are not mine.

Listen up—   they talk too much.
    Here's the trick—   there's no magic cure
        Take my advice—   you don't have all the answers

Symptoms of other people's lives
      when they came into trouble
           or figured it all out
        and that's great, it's good—
     but that doesn't mean it's for me.

I like to hear what they say,

    often there's something I can use
  now that I'm listening—hearing isn't the same thing,
        never was—
     but all that advice becomes its own fight
   a struggle between good intentions
          and good experience
  but when it comes at the expense of my self
     it's just not always worth doing.

Listen up— say something worthwhile.
  Here's the trick— you don't need to do what they say.
    Take my advice— for what it is, another option

Know that you make your own mind.
  Know that you have your own choice.
    Know that you live your own life.

Maker

Time is a funny thing
        when you have too little
                      everything matters,
      when you have too much—
                    nothing;
so my therapist said fill your time
          limit your free time
      idle hands
               lead to idle minds
      and idle minds
              lead to nothing.

I guess it's good advice—
              they seem happy
      busy doing something,
but I don't want to just do something
              to do it.

I want to create—
      bring something new into the world
              fixing what is broken—
          the car—my family—myself
                    seems like too much work
     and some broken things aren't worth fixing,
but to create to build—
        with my own hands
      to bring something new into the world—
                something that wasn't
                      becoming something that is—
        and looking at what you've created
      something new

        knowing that without you it wouldn't exist.

It doesn't matter
    if no one else would need it
            usefulness is not an end in creating
      because if it's something that you want
  and it doesn't exist—
        create it,
          then if for no other reason that you made it
     you will find a use
          for yourself
              your creation
      and it will matter to someone.

In that moment of creation,
          when the world stops
     and you keep moving
             and what wasn't moves closer to is
  you can forget the problems that you think you have
              because there is power
    in creating something you imagined.

```
Her
```

How do you know when you're ready for the spring,
when you're ready for the flowers and the birds
to once again begin to sing their elegant eloquence
in a symphony of light and scent and sound,
when you've been so deep in winter, in the desolate,
the cold wedded to your bones deeply engraved
in the senses of the times before you knew the world
was a place that could hold such beauty?

How do you know when you're ready for spring,
if all that you recall are the avalanches of last fall
when you let the world immolate innocent beauty
and sat laughing at the ashes of a past future,
and is it possible to find another play, another game
where those participating can keep themselves,
and no one has to burn in the crucible of time
where forgotten passions and broken promises turn to dust?

How do you know when you're ready for spring
with all her hopeful promises of warmth and thawing
of winters foibles set up like pigeons at a skeet shoot
to be blasted by the benighted rays of a life-giving sun
even though you cannot forgive the transgressions
of your past-self and let the future hold a promise
new sprouted from the frozen earth, its tender shoots
breaking the permafrost of another era?

How do you know when you're ready for spring
to accept the world as it is and not be bothered
by the weeds that were sown with the fresh lawn
because she knows that the errant seeds have come

with their own lessons and their own stories
and sometimes it's worth the effort to pull them up
even if their roots go deep and you know they'll grow back
because often the effort is its own reward.

Liminal Moments

My breath came up short again
      as I struggled to find the moment
the moment when my courage matched my task
      looking down the hall,
            clogged with students—my peers
    watching their screens—
        listening to their music—
not each other, walking without seeing.
        I see her.
She walks with her eyes awake
      seeing what others miss
          and missing nothing that they're seeing
and I know that she is different
            from me—from them—
      but it is a difference born of something more
          than what lives in the limits of my imagination
because she walks with her eyes looking—always looking
            for the world to step up
      and so I will try to step up.
I catch her eyes as they skate over the backs and tops of heads
         my heart beating over the rhythm of the feet
      and jostling of shoulders in a cramped hall
    that seems to narrow as she nears me—
        dumbfoundedly glued in place
      where I knew she would pass
although my place—my class—is on the other side of the school
            and even though I will be late
      and probably get in trouble
    it's worth it if her eyes land on mine for this moment
even if my will to speak—my breath is stolen by the siren
        her song unmistakable

                    the warmth of a future hope shrouded in danger.
          Our eyes meet over their heads,
and when she smiles,
                    it's not the distant vacant smile
                              of the constantly distracted
          but a smile that echoes the songbirds
                              whose nest sits snugly
               in the crook of the branches
                    outside the window of my room
it's a smile that wakes the rising sun
                    and knows that the world it moves through
          is more than a glowing rectangle in her hand.
Her smile stops before me, beatific in its grace
               to light on my thawing resolve
                         and before I can think of a reason not to speak
I ask the question that has burned my soul for weeks.
          "I was thinking—I don't know—wanna catch a movie,
     maybe hang out some?"
And in the benevolence of a spring morning
          when birds are the referees of those liminal moments before the sun,
                    in its celestial grace,
               shines on the dew encrusted morning
          her voice, honeysuckle growing in brambles of adolescence,
intones the answer that releases my entombed self-doubt
          wakes the elation
               of the dawn,
                    and she says yes.

Lift

I've been watching them for a month now,
        the baby birds outside my window,
    they wake me up in the morning
          but today the nest was empty.
    They'll be back, I'm sure,
  but for now they're out in the world—
          flying, exploring, risking
            their mother encouraging them to spread their wings
to find the breeze that will lift them
      from the dirt and branches
    into the sky.
           On my desk, torn into like a present on Christmas
      a present that has taken more to get—to earn
          than any I've had under the tree
    the envelope—fateful envelope: To the Parens of . . .
         spirited out of the box because I was afraid
afraid that it would condemn me
           take from me my wins of the past months
     each win wiping a cloud from the sky
     and opening up new possibilities
but in that envelope, now tattered and torn, is the prize—the pride
      of hard work, of a spring rain
          washing clean the last salt
  of an icy winter, opening the way for the tender shoots of the new
to find root in the once barren soil of a spoiled future.
      I open the window and breath in the fresh air, rejuvenated,
while the birds are singing to the sun.

Dirt Under Your Fingernails
My mother has always loved to garden,
but last fall, the weeds took over the planting beds,
and although she tried to find the time,
there was always something pulling her away.

Now I sit here, on the front step, looking at the grass
and I can understand why the façade was so important,
why she spent so much time cultivating the beds
and trimming the bushes that pushed their limits.

The cool lemonade, fresh squeezed and mixed
sweats in the glass on this warm spring afternoon
and while I'm tired and worn out, from helping her
the knees of my jeans stand with mud from the morning—

I've come to realize something very important:
It is often very good to get dirt under your fingernails.

June

The Bell

The anticipation grows
           with each silent tick of the clock
and while everyone knows
           the pantomime
    at the front of the room
                 is meaningless
we listen
      and watch
          and everyone goes through their motions.
I turned in my last paper for the year
         did my last worksheet
            answered my last multiple choice test
      and now—
        now—
I have just the silent time
            ticking away
      flowing through the room
                with a palpable essence
    pushing us unstoppably
                   to a future
as uncertain as out past
         but with one commonality
             one connecting sinew
      when that bell rings
               the final tolling of a tallied year
         we will be free.

```
Puddles
```

When I was little,
probably two or three
my mom tells me that I used to like
to jump in puddles.
She said that I would sit at the window
and watch the rain gather in the low places.
Once the rain lightened up
enough that she would let me go outside
I would run out
barefoot or in socks if she wasn't quick enough
and jump into the biggest puddles.
I'd come in drenched and shivering
with a smile that split my face in two.

I've outgrown puddles,
but standing on this rock
my friends yelling for me
to jump
while they swim in the pond below
I can't help but think about the stories
my mother used to tell me
about jumping into puddles.

Behind me, Ashley, my girl friend
laughs because she thinks I'm nervous,
I look back and she smiles at me,
the sun catching her eyes
and making her dark hair shine
almost purple with reflected beauty.

In that moment I realize how lucky I am

to have these people in my life—
to have my life—
and without turning back to the water
I smile and leap backwards off the boulder.

For a moment, in the air,
I'm weightless,
flying like the robins outside my window,
and I realize that these are the moments I was chasing
all along—
when gravity takes over
and the cold water
momentarily stealing my breath
washes over my head,
I smile
as I kick myself to the surface
to the cheers of my friends
and finally come up
into the sun.

Note from the Author

I didn't think this collection would be complete without addressing why this topic is so important to me. For many people who know me, my parents included, this may come as a surprise because I've told precious few about this, but when I was a freshman in high school, I seriously considered killing myself. I wrote a message on a sticky note, folded it up, and hid it behind the cork-board I had hanging in my room. That moment is still so vivid in my memory that I am a little teary remembering how close I came. The note said: "If I still feel this way in a year, I'll do it." I had kept it cryptic so if my parents found it they wouldn't know.

I have two loving parents who never had the problems that the protagonist's parents have; they were high school sweethearts who have made an amazing life for my sister and I, and now for their grandkids, and when it came right down to it, way back in high school, they were the reason I didn't just act on my impulse. I was picked on in middle and high school, nowadays people would call it bullying, but that wasn't the buzzword then that it is now. The thoughts and feelings of your peers matter when you're young. I realized, through that year, that suicide would hurt the people who loved me and who I loved, leaving them with a hole in their lives. I didn't want that for them, so I took a deep breath and pushed through and tried to forget about that little note hidden in my room.

When I found that note junior year in high school, life for me was very different. I was involved in the drama club at my school, I had a job I enjoyed, and I knew that there was hope and beauty even in the darkest moments. I lived, and still do, an amazing life with opportunity, loving friends, a supportive family, and now a fabulous wife and two beautiful children of my own.

Unfortunately, I've known people, children, who never got the chance to realize that our difficulties in life are so incredibly temporary. So I hope that this collection can help to reach someone in need of seeing that no matter how dark life gets for you, for any of us, that there is always a way to get back to the sun. Whether it's getting dirt under your fingernails or making something new or maybe just being with the people who lift you up, there is light even in the darkest moments. And when you think that everyone's back is turned, someone has their hand out to help you up. Just don't give up on yourself because someone, somewhere is willing to help.

I want to thank everyone for taking the time to share this journey with me. I know that some of the places we went were dark, but as a teacher for over a decade, I have seen these dark places in some of my students, some of the ones who are sitting in the back of the room or goofing off to get attention, and my heart truly goes out to them.

Author Bio

E.A. Johnson is a High School English teacher who has had the privilege of working with students in an important transition time in their life. While recently he teachers mostly seniors, he has worked with all grade levels at different times in his 15-year career. When he's not teaching, he can be found wandering in the woods looking for a good lake to swim in or playing in the back yard with his own children. And while they still get up in the middle of the night— nightmares are real—he wouldn't change a thing. You can find his previous poetry collection *The Conditions We Live* published by Unsolicited Press, You can find some of his other poems in The Chaffey Review (Spring 2010), The Battered Suitcase (Winter 2010), and Writing Tomorrow (February 2012). If you're looking for something a little different, he has also published a choose your own adventure story as an Alexa skill titled "Dream Weaver Unlocked." For more information or updates, check out his website: ericjohnsonwriter.com

About the Press

Unsolicited Press is rebellious much like the city it calls home: Portland, Oregon. founded in 2012, the press supports emerging and award-winning writers by publishing a variety of literary and experimental books of poetry, creative nonfiction, fiction, and everything in between.

learn more at unsolicitedpress.com. find us on twitter and instagram.